Charles Jones presents a clear-eyed and pragmatic view on the realities of corporate America that could make all the difference between someone thriving in any environment versus merely surviving a daily work-life existence. Charles reveals that it's all about one's approach and perspective. *The Company Doesn't Love You* is a tough love delivery full of real talk. Critical for today's workplace realities!

—Melissa B. Donaldson
SVP, Chief Diversity Officer
Wintrust Financial Corp.

Charles has courageously claimed the narrative of his personal and professional journey, filled with incredible highs and heartbreaking lows, in service to paving a smoother way for those who follow. There's a blessing here for those who are looking for a play book and a role model for successfully navigating life and career. So proud to call Charles my colleague and friend.

—Dorria L. Ball
President and Founder, Global Ballance Group LLC
Retired Vice President Human Resources, Mondelez Inc.

The Company Doesn't Love You: Be the CEO of Your Own Career is a must read if you are just starting your career, phasing towards retirement, and for every stage in between. This is NOT a book to read and put on the shelf, but to use as a guide. Charles shares relatable, real-life experiences that detail how to successfully navigate the life cycle of your career, focusing on the 5 Es and using the 'Life Fulfillment Framework' to serve as a compass. He nailed it!

—Treopia Cannon
CEO of Girls Inc. of Greater Houston

The Company Doesn't Love You takes the reader on an incredible personal and professional journey through the 5 Stages of The Career Life Cycle. Charles' deeply moving personal story and 25+-year meteoric HR career provide the insights and building blocks to help you successfully navigate the next move in your professional development and become the CEO of your own career! A must read for anyone looking for practical career advice presented in a thoughtful, humorous, and easy-to-follow way!

—Debra Basler
Banking Executive

Outstanding! Charles has captured the essence of what is on the mind and heart of so many professionals. The manner in which he captures the Life Fulfillment factors in a framework coupled with The Career Life Cycle gives a compass and a 'True North' for career growth. His experience, from working in the military as an officer to working in large corporations in HR, gives credibility and experience that can dramatically affect the lives of people for years to come. Well done!

—Corwin N. Harper, MHA, FACHE
Seasoned Healthcare Executive and Hospital CEO
Founder and CEO of 54forhumanity

Upper management in corporate America and education have a long history in celebrating up-and-coming professionals as they navigate through their career paths. The preponderance of published works to date acknowledges this timeless fact. This book builds upon and shows those up-and-coming professionals how to navigate the stages of their career life. Charles L. Jones, an experienced Human Resources Executive, shows throughout each chapter how to accelerate yourself professionally through your career path, accumulate knowledge, and build a successful career.

—Marcus A. Chanay, Ph.D., CFRM
Vice President for Student Affairs, Enrollment
Management and Campus Operations
Lincoln University of Missouri

Every so often a book comes along that engages the reader in a way that one can visualize themselves on the page and feel the emotions, triumphs, and frustrations the author is conveying. Charlie accomplished that with this book. In a very personal and affectionate way, Charlie provides a blueprint with practical solutions and thought-provoking ideas for one to navigate the multiple stages and emotional highs and lows of one's career.

—D. Crum
Vice President, Business Human Resources
AbbVie

Not often do you get a chance to pause and think about your career and what path you're on. This book provides amazing insight into every stage of life in the working world, and ultimately how we exit into retirement. We all fall into the trap of thinking the company will take care of us. The reality is, you need to take care of yourself. This book provides clear and concise recommendations and guidelines to achieve this goal, from someone who has vast amounts of experience in the HR world and has been exposed to thousands of people's careers. This read is well worth your time!

—Joe Wilson
VP Worldwide Sales
Ivanti

Charles reflects an excellent balance of values instilled within him by his parents and those he learned as a successful corporate leader: visionary, confident, decisive, effective in communicating, and embracing accountability—young executives or tenured professionals alike could greatly enhance their careers by reading this book!

—Micheal Cristal
VP of Operations, Kroger Corporation and International President of Phi Beta Sigma Fraternity, Inc.

Charles Jones really lays it on the line describing his experiences in the military and corporate America. I am glad that Chuck decided to be very transparent in his memoir, and I hope that his journey will inspire others. The views expressed are my own and do not reflect the official policy or position of the Army, Department of Defense, or the U.S. Government.

—Lieutenant General Leslie C. Smith
U.S. Army

A refreshing, pragmatic, and brutally honest insider's look at surviving and thriving in corporate America. This is a must-read for new graduates, those in mid-career, and perhaps most importantly, senior leadership in the public and private sector. True talent rises to the top, not because of your mentorship, but in spite of the barriers you have created to success.

—Marcia M. Anderson
Major General (Retired) US Army
Retired Federal Court Executive

The relationship between our emotional scars, our response to them, and the necessity of having a self-leadership mindset is expertly described by Charles L. Jones in his authentic, life-changing book. Jones shares his own journey with the reader and, in the process, teaches how trauma-inspired leadership begins when we recognize our pain and let it inform our purpose along the corporate or entrepreneurial path.

—Dr. Janet Taylor
Psychiatrist

This text provides a wonderfully insightful framing for career development and exploration. It speaks to a wide audience and provides relevant and timely wisdom on navigating the various stages of career trajectory.

Lamar R. Hylton, PhD.
Vice President for Student Affairs
Kent State University

Through his personal journey, Charles provides inspiration and insight for the recent college graduate to the seasoned executive. Along the career progression, he opens up about finances, family and faith. His story allowed me to better understand my own path as an executive, father and husband.

David A Turner, CPA
Chief Financial Officer
East Lake Management & Development Corp

THE COMPANY DOESN'T LOVE YU

Be the CEO of Your Own Career

CHARLES L. JONES

SB
PRESS

Published by StoryBuilders Press.

Paperback ISBN: 978-1-7341174-8-6. First edition.

I dedicate this book as a blueprint and playbook for those people who are seeking knowledge on how to successfully navigate the stages in their career. Even though the struggle is real, I hope it inspires you to believe in yourself and understand that the only courage you need is the courage to follow your own dream.

CONTENTS

CHAPTER 1

THE CEO OF YOUR OWN CAREER

I t was a hot summer day in 1975 in Magee, Mississippi, a tiny rural town an hour's drive from any sort of a city. Inside a mobile home just outside of town, an African American, no-nonsense mother scolded her ten-year-old son for his half-hearted effort on his daily chores. Again.

"Momma...I don't want to do chores! That's girls' work! I need to go outside!" With a firm but loving tone, she admonished him: "Charlie, you're lazy! You'd better go to college and get an education because you clearly aren't cut out for manual labor!"

Charlie ran out onto the porch and threw himself on the steps, crying as he confronted the realities of life. Frustrated, he thought about his options, but there seemed to only be so many career options available to an African American boy in that era: a preacher, a barber, a teacher, or a soldier. But this kid was different. He dreamed of more!

That same night, Charlie dreamed of himself as a grown-up. He had become an important leader in the community, a businessman wearing a dark suit and tie with round eyeglasses framing his face, a salt-and-pepper beard, and a really nice car—a wood-paneled station wagon! (For you younger folks, that's kind of like a souped-up minivan!)

In the dream, one of his neighbors called his name to give a speech to the community about his journey. The now grown-up, successful Charlie stepped onto the podium, happy to share all his wisdom and knowledge with the audience.

Charlie woke up the next morning inspired by his big dream. He jumped out of bed and searched excitedly for his father, eager to share his vision. His dad wore a few different hats in those days to provide for the family. He was a preacher, a barber, and had also owned a pool hall and a used car dealership. His busy dad paused to listen as young Charlie shared his dream.

Then his dad offered this advice: "Charlie, you have to know where you come from in order to know where you're going. You can go to college, get a job, or go into the military, but I know one day you're going to get out of this town and do big things!"

And Charlie believed him.

I know, because I am Charlie—Charles L. Jones. Almost half a century later, I've retired from an executive position in a Fortune 100 company after a 26-year fulfilling corporate career. That 10-year-old boy's dream came true, but in ways he could have never imagined.

It wasn't easy—far from it! My success in corporate America didn't happen by accident, and it wasn't due to luck or a company looking out for me. I wasn't on some secret fast track. There was nothing magical about my journey. But I did learn a thing or two along the way about the natural cycle of every career and how to navigate to success.

Did it involve sacrifice and dedication? Yes. Hard work? Absolutely. Some discomfort and failures? Sure. Good bosses and not-so-good bosses? Supportive colleagues and underminers? Of course. It had incredible highs, forgettable lows, and everything in between.

Yet I had the vision and a desire for more. I wanted to achieve that elusive American Dream by climbing the business success ladder. That dream has meant different things to different generations of Americans. It may mean something different for you as an aspiring leader, but for me, it meant succeeding against all odds as a poor African American boy growing up in Mississippi during the Civil Rights Movement.

And I believe that you—no matter your story or the odds stacked against you—can accomplish your career dreams, too.

News Flash: You Are in Control!

Maybe today you're just starting on a career path and could use some guidance as to what to expect. Or maybe you find yourself wanting to advance in your career but feel stuck and can't seem to jump the gap that keeps you from getting to the next level. You might feel held back by ethnicity, gender, family, personal challenges, your education or lack thereof, and any number of reasons.

Or maybe you just feel like your company doesn't care about you or your best interest. Well, here's a newsflash: Your company *doesn't* love you. And you shouldn't expect them to. It's not their job to manage your career—and that's good news. Your career growth, advancement, position, or any success you're going to achieve is 100 percent in your hands.

Does that surprise you? Does it shock you to think you have the ability to advance your career? How does it feel to know you're not at the mercy of your corporate circumstances, and the direction of your career is in your hands?

Maybe you can relate to a recent nationwide survey of U.S. workers that revealed 46% of workers are *dissatisfied* with their employment. Survey participants gave weak marks to the most important driver of job satisfaction: their current job's potential for future growth.[1] Do the math—that's almost one out of every two people who feels underappreciated, underutilized, just plain stuck, or trapped in a dead-end career. Other complaints included lack of communication, unfair pay, favoritism, overwork, micromanagement, and overbearing or incompetent managers.

Do any of these complaints sound familiar? Believe me, I get it. At one time or another in my career, I've felt the frustration of most of these situations. But as I reflect back on my experiences, I understand that every mistake, setback, and test I faced was necessary for me to take ownership of my career journey.

Been There, Done That

When it comes to climbing the corporate ladder, I've *been there, done that.* My career path began in military leadership before transitioning to corporate leadership, and it culminated in my becoming a Human Resources Business Lead for North America Sales with Mondelez International (formerly Kraft Foods).

That's a long way to travel for a dark-skinned African American man, born in the mid-1960s during the Civil Rights Movement and raised in rural and poverty-stricken Mississippi. For young Charlie, the odds of graduating from college, serving as an officer in the military during wartime, retiring as an executive from a Fortune 100 company, and starting a consulting business were, quite frankly, too far-fetched to imagine. It was simply taboo in those days to dare to dream big.

But I didn't let that stop me. I attended Jackson State University, a historical Black College & University (HBCU), on an ROTC scholarship. I joined that program initially thinking it was a way to get an easy *A*. I quickly learned that would not be the case, but I did work hard and graduated from the program with honors and a degree in finance. I was also blessed to meet my wife, Bobbie, a fellow finance major, during this time.

After graduating college I was commissioned a Second Lieutenant in the US Army and began my service. During my Air Defense Artillery (ADA) Officer Basic Course at Fort Sill,

Oklahoma, I was recognized as the top student of my class. Following that course, I was honored to serve in the Army's 1st Cavalry Division as one of only a few African American officers assigned there.

I was promoted to First Lieutenant in 1988 and assigned as the Executive Officer of a C Battery, 1-68 Air Defense Artillery at Fort Hood. As the "XO", I was second in command and assisted in the management of four platoons of Soldiers and air defense equipment. Part of that job involved writing battle plans, so in mid-1990, when the first Gulf War was about to begin (Operation Desert Shield, then Operation Desert Storm), my unit deployed to Kuwait as an advance party to develop battle plans, pre-position supplies, and handle other support logistics before the rest of my higher headquarters arrived.

In January 1991, I was promoted to Captain and assumed the responsibilities associated with commanding, leading, and managing soldiers. I returned to the US in September of 1991.

My first daughter was born only three weeks before my deployment to the Middle East for Operations Desert Shield and Desert Storm, so by the time I returned home, she had already celebrated her first birthday. With my new daughter in mind, I knew I wouldn't stay in the military much longer, because I recognized the stress it would create for my family long-term and didn't want that for my life.

I asked to be transferred out of the all-male combat arms units and into the Quartermaster Corps to stay closer to home. This unit more closely resembled the diverse makeup of corporate America, and I thought switching to this unit would better help me to assimilate into the *real world* and prepare for what I knew would be my exit strategy from the military. Within two years, I was offered a corporate leadership position.

After serving my country for six years in both peacetime and war, I began my corporate career with Kraft Foods, now Mondelez International. I was selected for a management training program that, combined with my persistence, hard work, and lessons learned that you'll find contained in these pages, resulted in a promotion approximately every two years.

Before I retired in 2018, I held ten positions of increasing responsibility with commensurate salary and benefits. In my final position, I was responsible for Human Resources Leadership for 5,000 sales associates and leaders across America and helped drive total revenue of $2.5 billion.

Your Career Life Cycle

In my work with Kraft, I spent a lot of time thinking about the product life cycle. When a product enters the market, it has a life cycle that carries it from being new and useful to eventually being retired out of circulation from the market. This process happens continually, taking products from their introductory stages all the way through their decline and eventual retirement. (Kraft's Trolli Road Kill, a fruit-flavored gummy candy shaped like flattened dead animals, is one example that sped through the cycle rather quickly.)

An *aha* moment happened for me when I realized that a career follows a similar cycle—but most people don't recognize it. Whether you are in corporate America, a small business, a non-profit organization, or even if you are an entrepreneur trying to build a business, the typical career has five career stages everyone must go through to succeed, whether at one company or—more likely—a number of companies.

I call it The Career Life Cycle, and the stages are: Exploration, Establishment, Elevation, Enrichment, and Exit (the 5 E's). I navigated each of the five stages while at the same company, but that isn't always the case for everyone.

As you assess your status at each stage of your career, you may need to course-correct when necessary, seek a new job, or make a career change, especially if you are a new entrant in the workforce with less than five years of experience. And there is always the reality that a company may not be a good fit for you at any stage. You have to be willing to be flexible but not run from challenges.

You have to be willing to be flexible but not run from challenges.

There is absolutely nothing wrong with exploring new opportunities and job-hopping as you pursue your career path. Remember, you are the CEO of your own career, so you get to make that call. However, the sooner you find your passion and locate the company that fits you and your goals the best, the sooner you can get established and build a foundation to jump-start your career.

If you're just starting out in your career, you may envision climbing that corporate ladder quickly, skipping rungs as you go, fast-tracking to the top. But there is a process to be followed to get there. When you understand the process, you can engage it with purpose.

When you understand the process, you can engage it with purpose.

You can prepare for the next stage and lay a foundation for a fulfilling retirement, rather than being forced into obsoletion and decline.

You can position yourself to live the life you want to live once your time in the corporate world is complete, while also enjoying every phase of your career journey by following these five stages:

1. Exploration

The Exploration Stage is the early employment time where people are typically in their early- to mid-twenties, have graduated from college, and recently entered the workforce.

At this point, it's about discovery, self-promotion, and individualism. Often, people create several fantasies and unrealistic expectations about what comes next. That's normal. But a common mistake

It's great to be confident, but equally great to embrace humility and realize you have a lot to learn.

made during this stage is to be impatient, subscribing to the "I Want It Now" mantra of instant gratification. No, you are not ready to lead the company immediately after graduating from college. You're not going to springboard to instant success as an entrepreneur. Your non-profit isn't going to change the world in a week.

It's great to be confident, but equally great to embrace humility and realize you have a lot to learn.

2. Establishment

At this critical stage, it's about applying what you have discovered in the exploration stage. You'll often be given opportunities to demonstrate learning agility, to make mistakes, to deliver results, to lead at different levels, and to receive promotions with greater responsibility. This stage requires you to build effective teams and achieve results through others. It's about the collective *us* and *we*, not *I* or *me*.

It's about the collective us and we, not I or me.

In some cases, you may be assigned a mentor or coach to assist in your career development and advancement—but not always. You may need to seek out support. Receiving feedback from others is important; if you don't, it's possible your development can be hindered.

In the corporate world, this stage usually starts around twenty-five years of age and covers about the next ten years of your Career Life Cycle. During this critical time, you'll plan ahead and take steps that look further down the road. For example, you might look into retirement planning, rather than postponing it until later in your career.

3. Elevation

At this stage, you've been in the game long enough to understand how it's played and should have earned a seat at the table. In most cases, it's simply unacceptable to consistently fail to deliver results or to add value to the company daily.

By now you should have clearly embraced the reality that you are the CEO of your own career. You should ask yourself where your ceiling is and what's your motivation. You've probably been assigned a sponsor and should have been placed on the Succession Plan to be promoted to at least two levels above your current salary grade.

If you've done the work, connected with people, and delivered results, you're probably considered to be high-performing, high-potential, and top talent at the company. If it's not working out for you, maybe it's time to consider employment elsewhere.

If you are an entrepreneur building your business, by this stage you need to consider how far you want the business to go and what systems, people, and processes you'll need to build to get there.

At this stage, it's essential to balance career and personal life, because it's likely a lot will be asked of you in both directions, creating competing commitments. Your retirement plan should be well on its way, utilizing wealth-building strategies like 401k, stocks, and personal savings.

THE CEO OF YOUR OWN CAREER

4. Enrichment

During the Enrichment stage, you begin to face reality. You should ask yourself how far it's possible for you to go. Usually, by this point, you'll reach the highest attainable position based on your career trajectory and promotability within the company. Unfortunately, in most cases, position and salary stagnation occur due to limited advancement opportunities.

For business owners and organizational leaders, it's time to start thinking about your exit strategy. As with every product, your Career Life Cycle is inevitable, so now is the time to prepare accordingly so you won't be pushed out by forces beyond your control.

If you haven't yet met with a financial advisor, it's time! By this point, you need to know your retirement savings goals in both the dollar amount and the year you're shooting for. A trusted and certified financial planner will help you make sure you're where you should be.

Also during this career peak, you should become a mentor to help guide others through their career experiences and challenges. At this stage, it's important to do reverse mentoring. Find that younger person who can also teach *you* a thing or two, enriching you with a new perspective. You'll also begin to prepare for life after your corporate career, laying the foundation for the post-retirement life you want to live.

5. Exit (or Decline)

You have a choice at this stage. You can either prepare to exit with dignity and on your own terms, or you can ignore the Career Life Cycle and slip into decline.

In the Exit stage, the decision has been made, either by you or the company, that it is time to part ways, voluntarily or involuntarily. If you're not prepared to step away from your corporate career or business and into what's next, this can be the most difficult stage, but it doesn't have to be.

As I'll share in the pages to follow, it certainly wasn't difficult for me because I had prepared for it, even though the circumstances weren't the ones I would have chosen. You may choose to retire, or you may decide to reinvent yourself to remain viable in the workforce.

The point is, by following the Career Life Cycle and the advice I'll give you in the pages to follow, you'll have the power to choose—because you are the CEO of your own career!

Achieving Your Highest Potential

Over the course of more than 30 years climbing the ladder in corporate America, I came to understand these five stages. I learned that there are key lessons, defining moments, and life-changing events that occur when you are chasing the American Dream—and they are transferable. You can learn them and apply them to your own journey, to pursue your own version of that dream. You don't need to live an unfulfilled life or be stuck in a career you don't want. With a little preparation and planning, you can control your own success.

Against all odds, I survived and conquered in my Career Life Cycle. That's not to say it was always easy, or that it will be easy for you. You'll need to make sacrifices, just as I did. But when you engage the process intentionally, you'll enjoy a satisfying and lucrative career, maybe at one company, but more likely across a few different companies.

> *You don't need to live an unfulfilled life or be stuck in a career you don't want. With a little preparation and planning, you can control your own success.*

It is my desire—my obligation—to pay it forward by sharing my journey from humble beginnings to career success, and the practical life experiences and lessons that shaped my professional path and personal fulfillment. In the pages that follow, I'll share practical life lessons, both empirical and anecdotal, that you can apply while navigating through the pitfalls and landmines of an ever-changing corporate battlefield.

If you apply the lessons I learned—sometimes the hard way—that are shared in the upcoming chapters, you will be well-positioned to achieve the highest potential in your own career.

You'll be able to measure your progress through each of the Career Life Cycle stages, avoid frustration, gain clarity on your direction, and ultimately exit on your own terms, financially secure and satisfied with a job well done. You'll be ready to enjoy the fruits of your labor.

Your career is in your hands, just as it was in little Charlie's hands so many years ago. But will you accept the responsibility to be the CEO of your own career? I hope so, because whether you realize it or not, you already are.

CHAPTER 2

THE COMPANY DOESN'T LOVE YOU

For more than twenty years, I seemed to be *the guy* at my company, the poster child for success and fast-track promotions. I moved up the corporate ladder so quickly you might've thought I was on a career advancement escalator.

In the first ten years of my career with Kraft, I moved from a basic, entry-level position for a degreed professional (Operations Supervisor responsible for fifty manufacturing employees) to the Area Human Resources Manager for the West Coast, responsible for manufacturing, engineering, and supply chain employees in six plants and four huge distribution centers.

Over the next ten years, I continued my climb all the way to the top—corporate headquarters in Chicago, where I ultimately became a Human Resources Business Lead for North America Sales. I was responsible for 5,000 sales associates and leaders across the country and helped drive total revenue of $2.5 billion.

But there was a personal cost to it all. I made sacrifices as I gave the best years of my life to the company. I relocated my family—frequently—all across the country. I also traveled regularly. (Although when I had to travel to one of the distribution centers in Hawaii, the trip didn't feel like a sacrifice!) I missed school plays, parent-teacher meetings, and often felt like I was on the outside of the special relationship my daughters had with their mother as a result of her playing the single-parent role so often.

And yet I can honestly say that my career success was fulfilling, even though there were significant tradeoffs. As one of the company's shining stars, I was well-compensated with salary, bonuses, and company stock (which allowed me to pay my daughters' college tuition)—so I assumed the company appreciated all my sacrifices and would always have my back.

In fact, it never occurred to me that it might be otherwise until 2013, when I came to discover a painful reality that everyone must know about the Career Life Cycle.

Trouble in Paradise

I had been with the company for twenty years. During that entire period, I hid the fact that I struggled mightily with some intense emotions, bouts of anxiety, and unexpected moments of anger. I couldn't explain my reactions, and trying to keep them under control left me feeling physically and emotionally drained. Finally, after one especially harrowing experience in a boardroom that year, I decided to see a doctor. That's when I learned the source of my struggle: PTSD.

I had been triggered on and off since my time in combat during the Gulf War way back in 1991, yet I never knew why. I'll share more of that story later, but imagine the relief I felt to know not only what was happening, but also that there was a weekly treatment program to help me manage the symptoms more effectively.

Of course, attending the program meant I had to be open with my boss to explain why I would need an afternoon off each week for therapy appointments. As a long-tenured employee and executive, that type of request generally isn't a problem, so I didn't foresee there being any issues.

I sat down with her the next day to share my diagnosis and explain my need for treatment. She was very supportive and, of course, allowed for my time off each week. I told her I wanted to share my diagnosis with my colleagues and staff in the department so they would know what was going on, too.

I clearly understood HIPAA laws and knew it was not a requirement to disclose my personal health concerns, but at the time, I felt it was the right thing to do. In some ways, it was a relief not to have to hide it any longer. I felt there was no reason to be afraid or to be in denial. It was a courageous and defining moment in my career. Even though this was a very difficult conversation, I felt it was necessary and the right decision for me.

At some point in your career, you will have to face your fears and challenges, too. There's no standard answer or solution. Therefore, I strongly recommend that you consult

THE COMPANY DOESN'T LOVE YOU

with your family, seek professional advice, and be willing to accept the potential outcome prior to disclosing personal and confidential information.

It wasn't long before I noticed a difference in how I was being treated. The company began to bypass me for promotional opportunities. I volunteered to lead large projects as I had done many times in the past; however, they would not select me to lead. I applied to open positions in the company for which I was qualified, yet I never received a follow-up nor any explanation regarding why I was not selected. In most cases, I saw the position was given to less qualified individuals. It seemed as if my career advancement came to an abrupt end after senior leaders found out about my PTSD. I will go into greater detail and provide lessons learned on dealing with fears, challenges, and obstacles in another chapter.

What hurt me the most was that I had opened up to them about my troubles, thinking they would understand, support me, and even leverage my reality for the good of the company. But that's not what happened. Instead, I felt like I was being separated from everyone else, almost pushed out. I was told, "Charlie, you can work from home." But I didn't want to work from home; I wanted to be in the office with people. I began to feel like they wanted me out of sight and out of mind.

Deep down, I could tell that the end of my stellar career run was near because they didn't seem to know what to do with me. In addition, I felt they were afraid of what could happen; they didn't want to be responsible or take a risk. I suddenly realized a painful truth that everyone must know, and the sooner the better: *the company didn't love me.*

For all those years when I felt like I was giving my lifeblood to the company, thinking I was *the man*, all the company saw was just *a man* getting an honest day's pay for an honest day's work—nothing more, nothing less. That was quite a wake-up call for me. I'd been believing the myth that companies really care. But in reality, that's not why they exist.

Luckily, because of intentional retirement preparations, I had already started crafting an Exit Strategy (Stage 5 of the Career Life Cycle). Consequently, when I was called into a meeting in 2018, told my job was being eliminated, and was handed a severance package to leave the company, I was neither shocked nor unprepared.

So now it's time for you to look in the mirror and ask yourself: *Am I under the same misconception that the company is looking out for me? Have I left my fate in the company's hands? Do I feel like the company or someone else owes me in some way?*

If you answer yes to any of these questions, you're in line with hundreds of thousands of employees everywhere. But because you have this book in your hands, your story is about to change.

It's time to step back, analyze your situation, and grab the reins to take control of your own career. No matter where you are today, you can decide where you want to be when it's your time to retire—once you realize that the company doesn't love you—and that's OK.

THE COMPANY DOESN'T LOVE YOU

Our Changing Workplace

In the early 20th century, career choices and advancement were often dictated by tradition, socio-economic status, family, and gender. For men, career choice—and status within those careers—was most often determined by what their fathers and other male family members had done before them. As I mentioned previously, in my family that meant being a preacher, barber, teacher, or soldier. For women, career choice options were even more limited by convention and social customs.

After World War II, corporate organizations became the driving force in American business. Both employers and employees operated under an implied contract: employees would be loyal to the company, and, in turn, employers would provide employment until retirement, which often included a comfortable pension.

Later in the 20th century, however, this traditional career trajectory of staying at one employer became a thing of the past. According to *USA Today*, the typical worker will have 12 different employers in his or her lifetime.[2] There were several factors for this shift, including the transition from manufacturing to a knowledge-based economy, that caused a decline in the implied contract of *employee loyalty for lifetime* employment. To get ahead or to make more money in today's business climate, employees often have to look outside their current place of employment. My long-term employment with Kraft was actually something of an anomaly for the 1990s and 2000s, and certainly would be today.

While traditional career ladders still exist in the 21st century, they operate within a different environment. For example, according to the Society for Human Resource Management, some of the new trends include…

➤ The way work is organized and performed continuously evolves and changes.

➤ Traditional career paths will continue to wane.

➤ Jobs are broken down into elements, which are then outsourced.

➤ Employees are working alongside a non-employee workforce lacking solid career paths and logical career progressions and may be harder to motivate.

➤ Workers value job enrichment, flexibility, and career development more than job security and stability.

➤ Work is redesigned to accommodate increased demands for flexibility, such as telecommuting hubs and online technologies for connecting with global colleagues and virtual worlds.[3]

Global staffing firm Randstad conducted a survey that showed 73 percent of employers said fostering employee development is important.[4] That's great, but the flip side is that only 49 percent of employees said leadership actually adheres to this practice.

In a traditional career ladder system, a person is hired, then through a combination of experience, education, and opportunity, he or she gets promoted to higher levels with additional responsibility and commensurate compensation. This progression within the same corporation continues until the individual retires, leaves the employer for another opportunity, reaches a level at which no further promotional opportunities exist, chooses to decline subsequent promotional opportunities, or is terminated.

But in reality, individuals are the CEOs of their own careers. They decide where they put their career ladders, how long they leave them in place, and how high they want to climb. Or, at least they do if they avoid buying into the following popular myths.

Myth 1: Yes-People Get Promoted

A *yes-person* is the one who endorses or supports every opinion or proposal of an associate or superior without criticism because they fear that, if they don't, they won't advance. Do you always stop what you are doing to assist a colleague with any problems? Do you always answer your phone on the first ring, no matter what you're in the middle of? Is your calendar jam-packed with meetings you really don't even need to attend? Are you afraid to express your opinion when you think it goes against what your boss thinks? If any of these sound familiar, you may have bought into this myth already.

I've observed people's careers going off the rails by trying to be that people-pleaser all the time. Admittedly, some company cultures actually seem to favor this sort of group-think on everything. In those instances, an employee may just be following the default company protocol for advancement. But even in those circumstances, artificially going along to get along is going to hurt you in the long run.

For one thing, many times when someone says "yes" but doesn't really agree, silent resentment grows just below the surface. This tension builds over time and kills morale. Then, when that frustrated person has had enough and finally decides to say "no" or to speak against popular opinion, he or she is perceived in a negative light. After all, something must be wrong, because there's never been any disagreement before.

> *Artificially going along to get along is going to hurt you in the long run.*

It's far better to honor your integrity at all times. Be courageous. Speak up. It is entirely possible to politely disagree with a colleague or manager, and, in my experience, your willingness to stand for what you believe is right earns you more esteem and respect than mild, disingenuous agreement. Of course, that doesn't mean your position will always be accepted, so you have to be okay with that, too.

> *It's far better to honor your integrity at all times. Be courageous. Speak up.*

Myth 2: You Have to Be Good at Everything

Another myth that relates to the yes-person problem is the idea that you have to know it all and be good at everything. People try to talk a good game to make managers think they can do it all and handle everything that comes their way—but when it's time to produce, they don't always deliver results. They overpromise and underdeliver.

When I was an Associate Human Resources Manager in South Carolina, for example, we hired a new employee over similar applicants because he was bilingual. We had many Spanish-speaking employees at this site, so having someone on our HR team who could help us with translation on certain special projects would be critical.

During his interview process, he said he could write HR strategies, workforce plans, compliance audits—you name it, he could do it. So I initially assigned him several easy projects to do, including an employee relations plan strategy to find ways to improve relations with our Hispanic community and improve their lives. But it quickly became apparent that he couldn't do it—any of it.

Don't inflate your skill sets. Be honest about your strengths and your struggles. If anything, underpromise and overdeliver, not the other way around.

When his 6-month evaluation came up, the decision was clear: he wasn't performing or delivering results, and, as a result, he was fired. I didn't have a problem with that because he had been dishonest about what he could do. He misrepresented himself as having more knowledge than he actually had.

Don't inflate your skill sets. Be honest about your strengths and your struggles. If anything, underpromise and overdeliver, not the other way around.

Myth 3: You Are Entitled to Quick Promotions

Another myth is that young workers can expect quick promotions. This false assumption has been popularized partly by young, ambitious college graduates, but also by the way companies present employment opportunities to this demographic. If you've recently graduated from college and are just getting started in your career, you are not entitled to special consideration or promotional opportunities because you graduated with a high GPA.

With Kraft, we had a process recruiting the best and brightest talent from key universities as they prepared to graduate. We would offer to bring them into a special program, giving them rotational assignments leading to high-level managerial positions. We let them know it was an opportunity to advance rapidly, and—this is key—we'd tell them the things *they* would have to do to make it happen.

The problem came a few months after they were hired— they forgot their side of the bargain. They would start to act entitled, behaving as if they believed they deserved to fly right up that ladder to join upper management in two years or less because they were the cream of the crop. That type of advancement would be an extremely rare exception to how the corporate world normally works, even in the case of specially-recruited young talent.

If you are new in your career and were put on a fast-track to management by virtue of your scholastic resume, recognize that you are probably moving at a faster pace and experiencing more than you would have with a regular, entry-level position. Then continue to do your part. Bring your A-game every day, in whatever situation you find yourself.

> *Bring your A-game every day, in whatever situation you find yourself.*

Where We're Going

Maybe at this point, you're thinking, *If the company doesn't love me, Charlie, why even bother? Why should I give my best to a company that ultimately doesn't even care that much about my success and advancement?*

I get it. Yes, I worked incredibly hard, sacrificing mightily along the way—and yet, I still believe that my experience was both rewarding and very much worth it. Anyone who intentionally designs and manages their career around the Career Life Cycle, no matter where in that process they are right now, will be well-positioned to enjoy a satisfying and successful career.

As a lifelong learner, I enjoy a wide variety of opportunities and learn a lot from them. With each move and promotion, I experienced working with different cultures, developed new skill sets, and learned to be confident in my own talents and abilities.

Several years ago, I was able to take advantage of my company's Education Reimbursement Policy. I went back to school, earned an MBA Degree, and the company covered my tuition.

When we accepted promotional opportunities, the company always provided a great spousal support process, which included resume writing and employment tips. And they would provide homeownership support by purchasing our home if it did not sell within a limited timeframe.

I don't regret any aspect of what I went through, not even my challenges and obstacles, because ultimately I learned. If you aren't willing to learn, or you're not willing to apply what you learn, you simply won't be successful. Equally important, I refused to succumb to the "I'm the victim" mentality. I

> *If you aren't willing to learn, or you're not willing to apply what you learn, you simply won't be successful.*

was not seeking nor expecting a handout from anyone; however, I always embraced and accepted a helping hand.

Nobody gave me anything. I had to prove myself each and every time. But those challenges and lessons made me stronger. They made my faith stronger and my story worth telling. As a result, I have been able to live my best life and live out my purpose.

Over my 20-plus years in a corporate career, I was able to be a positive role model. I impacted a lot of people, gave them opportunities, inspired them, encouraged them—and I really enjoyed that.

To go on a journey, it helps to have a compass and a map. If you don't have them, you could literally end up anywhere. In the following chapters, my intent is to provide you with the tools to craft your own career roadmap.

First, we'll unpack what I call the Life Fulfillment Framework that serves as a compass: Family, Faith, Finances, Fears & Challenges, and Friction. These five areas deserve special attention throughout your career and form the frame through which the Career Life Cycle makes the most sense. Then we will go deep into each of the 5 stages of the Career Life Cycle that can serve as your map for what lies ahead. I'll share my personal experiences and lessons learned in each stage and offer guidance to help you successfully navigate your own career experience.

So if you're ready to be the CEO of your own career—even knowing that the company you work for doesn't love you—then let's get started!

THE LIFE FULFILLMENT FRAMEWORK

CHAPTER 3

FAMILY

I was just three years into my career with Kraft's Oscar Mayer Business Unit in Madison, Wisconsin, and had already been promoted twice within that particular location. My wife, Bobbie, was working in her dream job as a marketing manager for American Family Insurance. Billboards across the state of Wisconsin featured her face. At the time, she was actually making more money per year than I was. My daughter was happy and settled into a good daycare routine—in short, life was good.

But then one morning the General Manager, who happened to be my mentor, tapped me on the shoulder for a promotion to Senior Financial Analyst with the Oscar Mayer Business Unit. It was an incredible opportunity, and I enthusiastically accepted the offer right on the spot. The problem was that the plant was in Newberry, South Carolina, a small rural town forty-five minutes northwest of Columbia, the state capital.

The full weight of that fact didn't sink in until I went home that evening.

When Bobbie got home from work, I met her at the door: "I think I have this opportunity in South Carolina," I started, choosing my words carefully, "and it's going to be for more pay and will position us to do great things with the company." Again I picked my words cautiously, "If I accept the job, they want me to be there next month!"

"Well, great," she said, "that gives us a little time, so let's think about it." I couldn't bring myself to tell her until the next day that I had already accepted the job.

"You did WHAT?!" (However loudly you read that line, go back and read it again, but ten times louder.) To say Bobbie was upset is the understatement of the century. I immediately tried to present my defense.

"Listen, it's my job as your husband and father of our child to be the provider. I'm asking you to allow me to be that provider. I need you to support this decision."

You can probably imagine how well that went over. Needless to say, the way I approached this particular situation was not a stellar example of how to effectively integrate family and career. The good news? It all worked out. I have a loving, understanding, and caring wife, and we made it through this bump in the road—and many, many others— by leaning into compromise, communication, and trust. I will go into greater detail in later chapters and elaborate on the importance of your spouse or significant other having a voice in critical decisions and to be a partner in all aspects of your career journey.

An Uncertain Start

It can be easy to overlook it, as I did at that moment in Wisconsin, but it's hard to overstate the importance of family in your career. At different times in the Career Life Cycle, you'll have different family concerns, and oftentimes these concerns are ongoing. In my case, I always had concerns at the back of my mind surrounding my decision making, how to juggle career and family, self-doubt, and questioning the stability and longevity of our marriage.

As a young man, I didn't have a clue where my life and career would end up. All I knew for sure was that I had to get out of Mississippi. I grew up knowing that staying home and living under my parents' roof as a young adult wasn't going to happen. So, while I didn't know what I was ultimately going to do, I did know I'd go to college.

I attended Jackson State University where I got my degree in finance. That's also where I met Bobbie, who was also a finance major. After I graduated in 1986, my next step was to serve in the United States Army, and so when Bobbie and I eloped in 1987, she became a military wife. I was stationed at Ft. Hood, where we had an exciting life but very little money. We were determined to make it work.

There was a lot of uncertainty—I might even say fear—at this time in our life. This was my first real job, and I knew I had to keep it to be able to take care of my responsibilities as a new husband and provider. With no extended family close by, it was just Bobbie and me. We had to learn how to depend on each other. We had to make it together as true partners.

Except oftentimes, we weren't *actually* together. When you're in the cavalry or infantry in the military, you're often not home. You're participating in field training exercises for several days or even several months. So it's important to have a close and trusting relationship. If you don't, the marriage is not going to survive. I would say the same is true for anyone starting out in a career and trying to integrate work and family life, but the military has an especially high divorce rate.

And then our first daughter, Tiffany, was born—a total game-changer. It went from being just the two of us to the three of us. How were we supposed to raise this child when we both had to work? We realized that one of us needed to become more of the homemaker, and the other, the primary financial provider. That realization proved to be a pivotal moment in the family, as was the fact that Tiffany was just three weeks old when I deployed to Iraq for a year during the first Gulf War. I didn't come back until she had already turned one.

Thankfully, the military is family-oriented. When a soldier is gone for months at a time, the military offers family support. Army wives are a tight-knit group, so Bobbie was able to get strong support when she started to feel overwhelmed. But missing a year of my firstborn's life did not sit well with me. I knew as soon as I returned from Desert Storm that I would have to make a change. That's when I began my journey into the civilian world and moved to Wisconsin.

We were fortunate to be part of the Oscar Mayer Division of Kraft, a company that, at the time, was also family-oriented. Their values and beliefs aligned with our family values. We knew everyone and felt like they were family. Bobbie knew other spouses with whom she developed friendships and a strong support system. The company hosted events every year, like Christmas celebrations and summer activities for kids, which helped make it feel like the right fit for our family.

Even as African Americans in Wisconsin back in the early '90s, when the minority population was less than 3%, we never felt different or like outsiders. The community and our church family warmly embraced us. Because of that family atmosphere and quality of life, Madison was listed at that time as one of the nation's top-five cities to live in.

However, one key to advancing with a company is being willing to relocate for promotions. We did eventually move to South Carolina with Bobbie's blessing, and she did finally adjust. It was there that our second child, Eryka, was born, and Bobbie made the decision to step away from her outside career and focus on raising our daughters. Her decision to stay home was difficult because she was educated, independent, and wanted her own career. She struggled with it to the point where it almost ended our relationship. She even harbored some resentment for a while. Eventually, it became a role she embraced wholeheartedly.

After a few years in South Carolina, I was tapped on the shoulder again, this time to move to California for promotion to Human Resources Manager. Fortunately, I learned my lesson the first time, so I knew to communicate about the opportunity with Bobbie on the front end before making any commitments. I promised her there would be more opportunities for the kids and a lovely house with a swimming pool. So off to California we went.

As we moved from place to place, moving upward and laterally within the company, we were able to put our girls in the best schools and social environments to be successful, which was such a blessing. And as we relocated, we enjoyed traveling, exploring, and adventuring out to new places as a family—we had a lot of fun!

During my time in California, I had to start traveling a lot for work because I was in charge of six different manufacturing facilities and three distribution centers. One tough pill to swallow was the realization that when I was out of town, I missed a lot of school and extracurricular activities, and all those little day-to-day encounters of family life. Life doesn't wait, and sometimes it was hard on the family that Dad was gone so much.

Sacrifices for Family

Overall, our family did love living in sunny, warm California, so when I was tapped on the shoulder yet again to return to "the frozen Tundra of Madison" (my manager's actual words), we had to have a serious family meeting. We broke out the pen and paper to list the pros and cons, the what-ifs, and everything else we could think of that would factor into the decision. Since Tiffany was 13 and Eryka was 7 at this time, we came to the decision as a family that the move was the right one to make, so I accepted. Four months later, when the school year ended, they followed me.

We re-settled into life in Madison, and two years later... you guessed it. I was tapped on the shoulder again and given the opportunity to work at our company headquarters in Illinois, bringing me as close to the top of the corporate ladder as I'd ever been. It was a lucrative position that would put me where I dreamed of being financially. But this time, the cost of moving the family was even more significant than the last.

So this time, with all the pros and cons in mind, Bobbie and I decided that instead of moving the family, I would make the sacrifice and commute to Illinois on a weekly basis, leaving on Monday mornings and returning home Friday evenings.

It was a two-year sacrifice we were willing to make for the kids, but it was hard on our marriage. I felt like I was missing a lot, so there were plenty of times I second-guessed myself. Yes, financially we were in a great place, but to be honest, at times it felt like a setback for the family.

If it had not been for our very intentional efforts at effective communication and active listening, I'm not sure we would have made it. First, we focused on our communication as husband and wife, and then together as parents. We checked in daily to make sure I was involved as much as possible with parenting decisions. Then, I'd call the kids if I needed to be loving, supportive, or sometimes strict, just to make sure they were OK.

The girls were at ages where stability was critical, with Tiffany starting high school. I did not want her to miss the opportunity to develop those close, formative friendships that develop during the teenage years.

As young adults today, Tiffany and Eryka have shared that, from their perspective, moving around so much as children had its benefits, but there were also some downsides. On the positive side, it made them more adaptable, raised their emotional intelligence, and helped them understand how to read people. Tiffany said that it made her feel very flexible in most situations and taught her how to roll with the punches. She also learned how to compete with the best and the brightest, gained from lessons learned along with every new move, which helped her become better at maneuvering and adapting.

However, each time we moved, the girls had to figure out how to join new social systems, especially as teenagers. Tiffany admitted that being young and having to navigate those systems provoked feelings of anxiety that she still has to deal with on occasion even today, especially with new or unfamiliar situations.

In the year 2000, with the intent of making sure our girls knew their voices were heard and their input was important to us, our family started a tradition on New Year's Eve that we carry on to this day. Every year, we turn off all TVs, computers, and everything else that might cause a distraction. We sit around the table and start with a prayer.

Next, everyone writes down on a piece of paper the things they've done really well the past year, things they didn't do so well, and things they want to achieve or do differently in the new year to come. Topics that are addressed can range from faith and relationships to career and life goals—whatever they want to focus on.

After giving everyone about 30 minutes to write it down, we all take turns sharing. We look for ways we can support one another with goals and habits, and we commit to practices we can all focus on as a family.

We place copies of everyone's sheet in strategic locations around the house: the refrigerator, bedroom dressers, mirrors—places where we can reflect on them regularly and honor the commitments we have made to one another.

This simple and meaningful activity we participated in as a family has endured now for 20 years. Even though the girls don't live at home, they make every effort to be home during the holidays so we can continue this exercise in family communication.

Over the years, we realized how important it is to keep a line of communication open with the kids when they needed to talk about a particular issue or problem. Bobbie and I each had instances of being that go-to parent, depending on what was being dealt with. When you enter that season of parenting teens, be ready to be available.

Were the sacrifices we made worth it? 100 percent! Today Tiffany is working as a Medical Doctor at Johns Hopkins Hospital in Baltimore, MD, and Eryka is an attorney in Washington, D.C. Bobbie and I couldn't be more proud of the young women they've become. It wasn't easy, as you can tell, but yes, it was most definitely worth it.

A Little Family Advice

How would I sum up the big lessons we learned about family and career for someone early in the Career Life Cycle? To start, and you can probably guess this, we tell everyone that communication is critical, early and often. Before you get married, have a conversation about what you are dreaming of for your life and career aspirations in 2, 5, 10, or even 50 years. Make sure you're on the same page.

Communication is critical, early and often.

When you're facing a major career decision, such as an upward promotion, lateral move, change of company, or even a total change of career, prepare your partner. Don't spring it on them like I did, or say "yes" without discussing it. Be proactive, and start communicating as soon as you see the possible change coming to limit the element of surprise.

As you communicate, work at aligning your priorities as a couple and as a family. When you agree on what is most important, it's much easier to filter opportunities that may arise to determine if one might be a good fit for your family's values and priorities.

Speaking of priorities, you can forget about work-life balance; it's a myth. Your real effort should be to develop work-life integration, where you make your work fit into your life, instead of functioning like a 50/50 balance was even possible. It's not. You'll never successfully split your work time and family time straight down the middle. Another consideration that requires attention is working from home. More companies are requiring employees to work from home rather than the traditional office space, which can be challenging to say the least.

Finally, as you're making a decision about whether to join a particular company, no matter where you are in the Career Life Cycle, always do your research to find out how that company treats the families of its employees. It's important to know if the company supports your family's values and beliefs. Do the company's values and priorities align with yours?

> *If you say family is your priority, don't compromise on that. Put the phone down. Turn the computer off. Spend time with them. The days are long, but the years are short.*

And one final gut check for you: If you say family is your priority, don't compromise on that. Put the phone down. Turn the computer off. Spend time with them. The days are long, but the years are short.

The bottom line is, for most of us, family is a significant factor in our career decisions and life fulfillment, and that's how it should be. The key is to intentionally integrate the two in a way that fully supports both key elements of life during every stage.

CHAPTER 4

FINANCIAL

I was a newly-hired Operations Supervisor with Oscar Mayer, fresh out of the military, when I received a call from John and Tom, two colleagues at the plant. The Plant Manager had assigned them to coach and train me. Neither had a college degree; however, both had over fifteen years of service with the company and were subject-matter experts in the meat production industry.

They asked if I was going to attend the town hall meeting later that day to learn about financial planning, personal investments, and 401k's. They also asked me what percentage of my salary I was investing in the company 401k.

I didn't know what to say, so I remained quiet. To be honest, I didn't know anything about 401k's and wasn't investing *any* money. Even though I had a savings account, I was living paycheck to paycheck and basically spending money as fast as I was making it. Apparently, and ironically, I was failing miserably at keeping up with the Joneses.

The topic of investing and saving became real to me that day. The guest speaker, a certified financial advisor, provided examples of how investing as little as 3% of my salary could lead to a huge nest egg and potential financial freedom over the course of a 20-year Career Life Cycle. As I looked around the room, it seemed as though someone flipped a light switch on in my brain. I understood the financial possibilities and became totally committed to becoming financially free.

The truth is, a large number of people today, if not most, struggle to make ends meet. In addition, statistics show a racial disparity gap exists when it comes to retirement savings. The average white family has over $130,000 in retirement savings, versus only $19,000 for black families. At that time, I was determined not to become a statistic.[5]

Early the next day, I walked into the Human Resources Manager's office and asked to speak with the Benefits Specialist. I immediately enrolled in the company's 401k plan and started investing 3% of my salary. Eventually, 3% was increased to 30% over the course of my career. In most cases, instead of spending my annual salary increases, I simply increased the percentage of my 401k.

The commitment that I made to myself to save and invest required exceptional discipline and unprecedented professional maturity, which was mastered over time. And it paid off in a huge way when it was finally time to exit my career.

Lessons from Dad

The financial lessons we all learn, good or bad, start in the home at a very young age. One of the first things I learned was the difference between a *want* and a *need*. Growing up in poverty, I knew we couldn't afford to buy fancy things, so I learned how to live within our family's means. Looking back, I realize now that I learned to appreciate and be grateful for the things I actually *did* have.

With my dad being a pastor, there were some financial lessons we learned from the Bible. One of his favorite lessons came from the Parable of the Talents in Matthew 25: 14-30, where a master, while away on a trip, puts his servants in charge of his talents (monetary units). Upon his return, the master reviews the stewardship of his servants. He judges them according to how faithful each was in making wise investments of his talents to gain a profit. The master rewards his servants according to how each has handled his stewardship. He judges two servants who invested the talents as having been faithful and gives them a positive reward. To the single unfaithful servant, who played it safe and buried the talents, he actually gives a negative compensation and takes what he has away from him.

Whatever you get in life, whatever you have in life, cherish it, but don't just sit on it.

This lesson taught us that whatever you get in life, whatever you have in life, cherish it, but don't just sit on it. Figure out how to make things better for yourself and other people. In this way, I learned how to take wise risks and give back what I had been given.

As a result, I believe in giving back to the church and to the community. Instead of storing up all the treasures over the years, we gave back. And the more we gave back, the more these treasures kept coming to us. Money has continued to come in all these years.

Dad taught me about money in other subtle ways, too. For example, when I was in middle school or high school and needed money for a school expense, he'd ask me to get the money I needed out of his wallet. He wanted me to see that he had money there. In his mind, it seemed to be his way of encouraging me or inspiring me to get money of my own. And it worked! *Wow! Look at all that money!*

My dad was also a salesman for hair care products at one point. He would drive around in his Volkswagen on Friday afternoons and all day Saturday, letting my brother, Julio, and me ride with him on his routes to beauty salons and barbershops. I'd see the beauticians and barbers paying him cash for the products, which he'd put in a bankers' bag. At the end of the day, he'd have Julio and me count all the money.

Then he'd teach us how it all worked. Let's say he made $500 that day. He'd write that amount down, then list the bills that had to be paid and have us do the math. If that left $150, he'd say, "Ok, you take $10, and we'll put the rest in the bank." In this way, he taught us about the connection between money, wisdom, and hard work.

Of course, I did not necessarily appreciate these lessons when I was learning them. I didn't always like my parents when I thought they didn't give me what I wanted. But I learned the value of a dollar. To this day, I don't spend a lot of money, and neither does my wife, Bobbie.

Bobbie came from a family that struggled financially even more than mine did. She grew up in the Mississippi Delta in a family with seven children. They had very little. There simply was no money to manage. Bobbie's mother passed away when she was four, so her dad and sisters raised her on his income from working on a farm. She didn't know about managing money or finances until she went to college, where she majored in finance, just as I did. So the potential for a lot of misunderstandings about money existed when we got married.

Start Small. Start Now.

When we first got married, Bobbie was working, and I was in the military. We had two separate bank accounts, and yet it seemed like the money was evaporating. What we quickly learned was that when a family has one unified account, it can be managed better. With two accounts, there are going to be some leaks. When we began to take care of our finances out of one account, we started to see a light at the end of the tunnel because we developed a sound spending structure.

When I went off to war, I received hazardous duty pay. That meant I was making a lot of tax-free money. But while I was out there on the battlefield, it got real and rough. My life almost came to an end at least three times. I promised myself that if I ever placed my feet back on US soil, I would buy myself a nice car. Thank God, I made it back alive. To keep the promise I made, I went ahead and bought myself that car. To this day, I hate to say I did it, but because I made myself a promise, I felt like I owed it to myself.

While I was gone, Bobbie had saved a lot of money. She tried to talk me out of getting the car. I really put up a good argument though. Finally, with her reluctant consent, I bought a brand-new, 1990 Black Porsche 911. *What was I thinking?!*

She justified the purchase in her mind by telling herself that we were doing well at the time; we were young and could recoup the money that we had saved. I think we put $8,000 down on the car, which cost around $30,000. Back then, that was a lot of money for a car!

It didn't take long for me to realize the car was a liability that placed a financial burden on us. A Porsche is a *nice-to-have,* but not a *must-have.* But I looked at the whole thing as a learning experience. From that point on, every car we had, we kept at least 10 years.

After I left the military and was recruited to work for Oscar Mayer in Wisconsin, our lack of planning nearly put us in deep financial trouble. One of the appeals of this new job was that I would make more money—significantly more. However, we failed to take into account that we got additional money in the military for certain costs of living, like rent, groceries, etc.

We weren't factoring in any of that, so when we moved to Wisconsin and got my first paycheck, Bobbie said, "I think they underpaid you! You need to go to HR and ask where the rest of your money is."

So, I dutifully went to HR and asked, "Can you make sure my paycheck is right?" They did all the calculations, and guess what? It was right! I gave them my military pay stub and my Oscar Mayer pay stub to compare, and they told me I didn't take into consideration state taxes and the additional military stipend I received every month. Lesson learned.

We thought we were about to live the high life, but in reality, we went backward financially in the move. Because we had overestimated our finances coming in, we had issues paying the bills. Although we stumbled coming out of the gates, we learned from it. I learned to research the cost of living in the next place we moved, and for every move thereafter, which wasn't an easy task back then. Now, you can find a ton of websites featuring cost of living comparisons for everything from gas to utilities to the housing market, so you can make an informed decision.

On our next move to South Carolina, I made a different financial mistake: I failed to factor in whether my wife would be able to find employment in a new location. Bobbie was working for American Family Insurance at their headquarters office in Madison, Wisconsin, so she had to give up her job, relocate, and try to find another job that fit her career experiences and degree. I simply assumed it would all work out. When it didn't, we were once again struggling, living paycheck to paycheck.

It all came to a head one summer when we were driving from South Carolina to Mississippi, bringing our daughters to see their grandparents and extended family. While driving, the car broke down. At this point, we had three credit cards, two of which were maxed-out. There was just enough credit on the third card to get the car fixed, and we still had to stay somewhere overnight. That's when it hit us that we couldn't keep living that way. We needed some financial margin.

We dropped the kids off, drove back to South Carolina, then sat down and looked at our finances. Here we were, two finance majors who were failing miserably. We wrote down every bill that we had, every single expense. Then we wrote down the revenue coming in and realized we were falling short. We decided that if we consolidated our bills, getting a consolidation loan from USAA, we would be better positioned to pay the bills and put us back in the green on a month-to-month basis. The process forced us to sit down and analyze money coming in and money going out, and think about options in an intentional way. We both agreed that the best option was to take out that loan and pay off the bills. That structure actually helped us become debt-free over time. Every year we would decide which one or two bills we were going to pay off, typically the ones with the highest interest rates first, and then we would cut up that credit card.

We did take a small step backward when we moved from California back to Wisconsin. We wanted to buy a new home and needed $50,000 for a downpayment. At that career stage, we didn't have a lot of savings, but we had a lot in my 401k. I definitely do not recommend doing that now, but we went into our 401k and took out the money to use as a downpayment on our home in Madison. We took a step back, but eventually made money on the sale of the home and paid back our 401k.

Years later, when it came time for Tiffany to go to college, we didn't have enough money saved to cover her costs. When we first had Tiffany, the friends and colleagues we met early in our marriage talked about how they set up college funds for their kids.

It's important to start small rather than not to do anything. You have to start somewhere.

So we set up a 529 savings account through USAA with $50 a month. We knew it wasn't enough to have a big impact, but we started small and felt good about it. Every year we put more and more into the account. And that's the key: it's important to start small rather than not to do anything. You have to start somewhere.

Luckily, Tiffany earned an academic scholarship. We were in that middle stage of our career, and just beginning to see some financial light, so we couldn't give her the same financial support we were later able to give her sister. While Eryka didn't get a scholarship to the school she chose, by that time we had saved enough money to pay for her schooling. She was able to go to school without a student loan, which we were glad about.

> During your journey, you will eventually understand that it's not where or how you start; what matters is where and how you finish.

The lesson learned here is to start early—save and invest as aggressively as you can, so you will be fully funded when the time comes. During your journey, you will eventually understand that it's not where or how you start; what matters is where and how you finish.

Ask for Help

As I shared in the beginning of this chapter, my 401k savings efforts started at the beginning of my civilian career, when I was barely making ends meet. But I was convinced that getting started was vitally important, so I began with a small contribution of around 3%.

Five years later, when I was in California, I reviewed my 401k financial statement: *WOW! That's a lot of money!* I hadn't actually realized how quickly a 401k would grow when properly managed, even with such a small initial investment.

Bobbie and I came to realize that we could really work toward a comfortable future—and maybe even early retirement. So from then on, every time I got a promotion or a pay raise (usually 2.5 - 3%), I wouldn't spend the money. We would just add it to the 401k. By doing so, we never missed what we never had. By doing this, we were living below our means but never felt the lack. We continued saving in this way until eventually 25 - 30% of my salary was being invested by the time I retired at age 53. I am not suggesting that everyone can afford to invest 25 - 30% of their salaries into a 401k or Retirement Fund. However, I am recommending that you set a lofty goal to invest the maximum percent allowed as early as possible in your career.

One key topic that my parents never talked about with me was intentional financial planning, and that's just because it wasn't something they were familiar with. I believe that financial literacy has a direct correlation with financial success, especially when it's learned and put into practice early in your career. However, financial literacy among African Americans is low, which is primarily due to significantly lower upward economic mobility. African Americans make up 13 percent of the U.S. population and constitute a critical segment of our economy. Yet financial literacy gaps exist across this demographic regardless of gender, age, income level, or degree of education.[6] In my conversations with those older and wiser colleagues who were further down the road than I was, I came to understand the importance of bringing in someone who is completely versed in financial literacy and options.

As a result, in 2003 Bobbie and I decided to hire a financial advisor in California before we went back to Wisconsin. By that point my salary was strong, and I was getting great bonuses and stock in the company. Because we didn't know on our own how to get the greatest return on our investments and prepare for retirement, we hired an advisor with Ameriprise Financials. Not only did we enhance our knowledge of investment and financial planning, but we also opened accounts for our daughters and educated them on the importance of financial literacy. It was the best decision we could have made.

When you're ready to do the same, probably somewhere in the Elevation stage of the Career Life Cycle, start by asking around in your network for recommendations. We were fortunate to find someone who was well-grounded, certified, and entrenched in the community, but we interviewed three possible advisors before making our decision. Make sure to choose someone you can trust who has a history of being successful and honest, and who works with a reputable company.

In the chapters to come, I'll share specifics of what to do financially at each stage of your career. But perhaps the key takeaway here is not to let ignorance or fear stop you from being intentional about your finances. Remember, you are the CEO of your own career! The company doesn't love you. So take charge of your own financial future and freedom.

CHAPTER 5

FEARS & CHALLENGES

E veryone experiences fears and challenges they must deal with. It's never a matter of *if* you'll have something significant to deal with or *if* things won't go as expected; it's a matter of *when*.

Sometimes these fears and challenges come from the outside world, but each of us brings our own inside baggage with us as well. These internal challenges can derail us if we aren't proactive about dealing with them. Some are physical, some emotional. Some people deal with significant family challenges that bleed into the workday; others have interpersonal issues with colleagues that make it difficult to properly perform.

These internal challenges take many forms in the Career Life Cycle and often surface in unexpected ways. For me, one of my most significant challenges crystallized when I was promoted to my first Kraft Corporate Headquarters role as Associate Director HR Global Supply Chain in March of 2006.

The new position required relocating from Madison, Wisconsin to Libertyville, Illinois. I was now responsible for strategic staffing, diversity, training, and university relations for North America, which consisted of over 29,000 employees and 60 manufacturing plants. As often happens when someone starts a new position at this level, I didn't get much help; I was simply expected to figure it out.

I had to attend a weekly, cross-functional senior leader staff meeting which included Vice Presidents and Senior Directors. During the staff meetings, I provided updates on hiring, recruitment, and diversity in North America.

In April 2006, just a month into the new role, Mary, my new manager, asked me to provide a staffing update at the meeting and also offer a hiring forecast for the upcoming quarter. My stress and anxiety levels were rising rapidly and spinning out of control. I had been hired for the position over the objections of an individual who wanted someone else to have the job. I didn't fully realize it at the time, but that person was working against me as I got started, often undermining my efforts by withholding information or help.

So as I entered that meeting, I knew I had a lot to prove in the new role. Even though I was top talent, a high-potential and high-performing leader, I feared being embarrassed or having an anxiety attack triggered by feeling irritated, upset, and constantly on guard. Based on previous experiences in my career, which I'll explain later in this chapter, I was concerned I wouldn't be able to control my behavior or emotions. Most importantly, I feared losing the job I needed to take care of my family.

In that April meeting, I was the second or third presenter. All the North America Global Supply Chain Leaders sat in the conference room around a table looking at me, the new guy. I knew some of them didn't want me to have this particular role. However, while presenting, I was confident as the subject matter expert, comfortable, thoroughly prepared, and anticipating some difficult questions. I felt really good about my delivery and the meeting outcome. My presentation went well; however, during the Q & A session, the unthinkable happened.

Some of the questions they asked began to trigger stress and increase my anxiety levels. I felt I had been set up to fail. I could sense I was getting angry. For some reason, I felt they were targeting me and singling me out. Due to the tension with the other person who wanted the role, I already struggled to trust anyone because I didn't know who wanted me there and who didn't. My emotions began taking over. I could feel myself starting to lose control. I struggled to concentrate. My heart began beating faster and faster. My hands began to shake. Sweat began to drip from my brow. I felt lightheaded, like I was going to pass out.

I somehow managed to keep my composure long enough to say thank you to everyone. But when I sat down, the sweating and lightheadedness kept getting worse. I remember a colleague asking if I was feeling ok. I said yes, but then politely left the conference room and ran to the men's restroom. Thankful that no one else was there, I ran into an empty stall, stripped down to my underwear, and laid on the tile floor to cool down. My body was simply soaked with sweat.

After about twenty minutes of lying there, I began to feel normal. I didn't know if anyone witnessed what had just happened. I quickly dressed and went to the sink to splash cold water on my face. I was so afraid; I actually thought that I was going to die. I didn't know what happened to me or why. However, I knew something was not right, and I couldn't control it.

I was confused and lived in fear of this experience happening again. Years later, in December 2013, I received a diagnosis of Post-Traumatic Stress Disorder (PTSD).

What I discovered was that my personal challenge stemmed from my time in the Army during the Gulf War. For years, I had dealt with PTSD but never knew it. I did know I could be triggered into angry outbursts for the smallest reasons, and I spent a significant amount of time and effort controlling my emotions and behavior. As a result, I often noticed I was overly nice or worked hard to stay in a pleasant or good mood because I didn't want to be triggered.

Your challenge probably looks different, but some of the key lessons and takeaways I learned from dealing with my challenge may be helpful to you as you progress through the Career Life Cycle. In sharing my PTSD story, I hope to help you to draw parallels to your own unique situations and consider ways you might best navigate them.

My PTSD Journey

It was in 1991, a few days after returning to my home base at Ft. Hood from Operation Desert Storm, when a loud thunderstorm startled me out of my sleep. I woke, drenched with sweat, with my heart beating fast and my hands shaking. I jumped out of bed and onto the floor, mistakenly thinking the noise and flashing from the thunder and lightning was gunfire. My frightened wife didn't understand what was going on. Neither did I. But for the first time, I suspected something was wrong.

> It was in 1991, a few days after returning to my home base at Ft. Hood from Operation Desert Storm, when a loud thunderstorm startled me out of my sleep.

When I left the military, there was no counseling or therapy or anything like that available to us during that time. We simply turned in our guns and ammunition and walked out. For the next twenty-two years, I continued to experience really bad dreams. As a result, I had difficulty sleeping and always felt fatigued. The dreams were mostly about mistrust, dying, killing, and having a feeling of guilt for those who were killed in Iraq. I felt I could have done more as an officer. I could not watch military movies or documentaries, was always on edge, and felt like I lived every day with a short fuse. I didn't like being in public places or around a lot of people, especially those I didn't know or couldn't trust. I knew something was wrong, but I was in denial, ashamed, and embarrassed. Unfortunately, for several years I subdued the feelings and coped by self-medicating with alcohol.

Still, from time to time the PTSD would surface unexpectedly. In 1999, while living in California, I went to a hardware store with my family. I would usually stay in the car while they shopped, but on this particular day, I decided to walk into the store with them. I took a few steps inside the store, but the large crowd was too much for me to handle. I felt like everyone was watching me, and the people were moving faster and faster. My heart started beating fast, and I became lightheaded. As I walked out of the hardware store, a car didn't yield while I was walking across the street to my car. And I got very angry.

Everything turned black as my world went totally silent and dark. When I regained my composure and awareness, I had jumped on the person's car, screaming and shouting while punching the windshield. Bobbie hollered, "Stop! Please, stop!" She grabbed me and pulled me into our car. She was crying while we drove out of the parking lot. It was a strange feeling because it was almost as if everything just got dark, went black, and I didn't really remember anything.

After Bobbie calmed me down, I was breathing hard, sweating, and shaking. I was scared because I didn't know if I had hurt someone or if someone had hurt me. After the incident, the entire day was quiet around the Jones house, as we were all wondering what had actually happened. I just knew that something was wrong with me. We never really talked about it, so eventually, the incident faded away and got pushed to the background. I basically wrote it off as some type of fluke. I hadn't been diagnosed, so this was all new to me.

Another incident happened in 2008 when I was asked to join a University Relations Recruiting Team for an event at Lincoln University in Jefferson City, Missouri. After checking into the hotel, I walked downstairs to wait for colleagues to pick me up. While I was waiting, a guy walked into the lobby, looked at me, and made what I thought was a smart remark. Feeling challenged, I asked if he knew me. He said he didn't know me and didn't care to. That's when I lost it.

I flew into an angry outburst and grabbed the guy. With my heart beating rapidly and hands shaking, I felt lightheaded and started sweating profusely, and that's when I finally realized my emotions were out of control. I released the guy and ran up to my hotel room. I got to my room soaked with sweat and thought that I was going to pass out. I took my shirt off and laid on the tile floor in the restroom to cool down. After about thirty minutes, I got control of myself and met up with my colleagues, a little late, but no one else knew what had happened.

To be candid, for all those years, I just thought I was mentally ill. After returning from the Gulf War, soldiers were not educated on identifying and understanding the symptoms of PTSD. The military did not provide mental or psychological sessions. Mental health support and assistance did not really exist in the military at that point in time. We pretended everything was OK, behaved as if there was nothing wrong. After all, real men don't admit when something is wrong—at least not until there's no avoiding the reality of it.

Finally, in 2013, I saw a doctor and received the diagnosis.

"It's Going to Be Ok"

As I shared earlier, my treatment involved weekly therapy sessions, so I had to tell Dorria, my boss, what was happening. I asked if I could share my diagnosis with colleagues and staff in my department rather than trying to conceal it from them. I had known Dorria for several years; she was a caring and respected leader with high integrity. She said, "Charlie, you know that you don't have to say anything about this to anyone. You have my total support, and I'm here for you."

At the time, I knew that I didn't have to disclose my medical condition; however, as a leader, I felt the right thing to do was to be courageous and unashamed to open up to my colleagues. At this point in my career, I was in the Enrichment stage with twenty years of service in one company. I felt that I had nothing to lose and needed to face my fears. For those of you who are in the early stages of your career or think you have too much to lose, I recommend that you consult with your family and a physician or therapist, and clearly understand where you are in your career prior to disclosing personal medical conditions to your employer.

For the next few years, I continued to manage my PTSD symptoms when they would come up during the workday; at least I had some counseling and more effective coping mechanisms. But it wasn't easy. In fact, sometimes it consumed me.

For example, when I was in a meeting in 2015 with other colleagues, one of them said some demeaning things to me. Dorria saw the expression on my face, which probably indicated, *I'm about to lose it right now!* But I had learned what to do: I counted to 10 and intentionally focused by slowing my breathing. I felt like everyone was observing me. It took a lot of effort to control my response, and I was mentally exhausted. After the meeting, Dorria asked, "Why did you let him talk to you that way?" I replied that I had been triggered, and it took every ounce of energy in my body not to have an outburst.

I would often intentionally smile or pretend to be happy because that's the perception I wanted others to have of me. When I went to work every morning, I'd pray the whole way, *Please don't let me have an outburst. Please don't let me be triggered.* I'd walk in smiling and joyful, but I had to consciously put myself in that place every day. It was exhausting.

As I shared in Chapter 2, I had begun to notice I was being treated differently. Where I had previously been on the fast-track, the company began to bypass me for promotional opportunities. I would volunteer to lead large projects, which I had done many times in the past, but would not be selected to lead. I would post for open positions I was qualified for in the company, but I never received a follow-up nor any explanation as to why I hadn't been selected. In most cases, they would give the position to less qualified or experienced individuals. To put it plainly, it seemed as if my career trajectory came to an abrupt end after senior leaders found out about my PTSD diagnosis.

Finally, in early 2018, I co-led a Leadership Symposium in Nashville, Tennessee. Invitations had gone out to over thirty-five senior leaders.

A group of ladies was first on the agenda to speak and accept large food donations from Mondelez International. They were members of Blue Star Mothers, ladies who talked about their sons and daughters who did not return from Iraq and Afghanistan. As they talked about the importance of serving the country and being prepared to sacrifice your life if required, I could feel my emotions taking over.

My heart once again began to beat fast. The sweating started. My hands began to shake as I felt lightheaded. All of a sudden, as I leaned against a wall near the ladies, tears began to roll down my cheek. I couldn't stop them. The ladies' voices seemed to get louder and louder. I kept thinking back to the Gulf War and those who had made the ultimate sacrifice.

I quietly walked out of the meeting to get some air and regain control of my emotions. I thought I was walking alone down the hall, when someone behind me said, "Charlie, it's going to be OK." When I turned around, it was Matt, a Senior Executive. He had followed me out of the meeting room. Matt and I gave each other a big hug. After I got myself together, we walked back into the room. For the first time, other senior leaders in the company outside of my immediate circle knew something was wrong. I couldn't control it, hide it, or cover it up anymore. Later in the day, several other senior leaders found me and asked if I was OK.

The Beginning of the End

I knew this was the beginning of the end of my career in the company. By October 2018, I had been offered a severance package. My last day in the company was December 31, 2018.

It took a couple of months for me to accept the fact that I had given the best years of my life to the company, and even though I knew the day was going to come, the reality of leaving it was different than the theory. Interestingly, I had planned ahead and estimated what year I was probably going to be offered an early retirement package—2018. So the timing didn't surprise me.

What hurt me was that I had opened up about my challenges to my colleagues, thinking they would understand, support me, and leverage it for the good of the company. But that's not what they did.

At first, I felt that they tried to distance me from everyone else. "Charlie, you can work from home," they said. But as I said earlier, I didn't want to work from home. I wanted to be in the office with people. I get it. Unsure what to do, I assumed that was their way of minimizing risk, moving me out of sight, out of mind. But it was hard.

I became depressed. Even though I was taking medications for PTSD and anxiety, I shifted back to some old ways and began drinking again to try to cope. About six months after I left, I knew I had to get myself together and started working my way to a better place.

Today, as I look back, I think things might have gone differently for me if I were to experience these same issues in the current workplace. It seems companies are more accepting and better educated about PTSD and mental health. In addition, most companies provide support and assistance through Employee Assistance Programs (EAP), as well as Affinity Groups within the company. However, unconscious biases, micro-inequities, and microaggressions exist in every company, and people often unknowingly treat you differently or single you out because these biases have gone on for so long.

In general terms, mental health can significantly impact a person's career. It shapes how co-workers and senior leaders perceive you, especially those who decide the trajectory of your career and promotional opportunities. If you struggle with anything related to mental health, whether that is PTSD*, anxiety, bipolar disorder, depression, OCD, ADHD, or anything else, I recommend first seeking medical help and then speaking with a trusted mentor or colleague at work *if* it would be helpful for someone there to know your situation. It isn't necessary for you to broadcast your problems widely, and in fact, in my experience, that can have negative consequences.

But don't be afraid to share your challenges or ask for help from the core people you trust.

Mental health is not the only personal challenge you may have to deal with over the course of your career. It certainly isn't the only one I faced! Lack of conscience, fears, anxiety, pressures at home, physical ailments—the list is *Don't bury your problems and just hope they'll get better.* nearly endless. The bottom line is, you need to expect to encounter struggles and be prepared to acknowledge and address them. Don't bury your problems and just hope they'll get better. If left unaddressed, it will eventually undermine your Career Life Cycle and leave you feeling unfulfilled, no matter what title is on your office door.

*Please see the Special Note about PTSD at the end of this book from Dr. Janet Taylor, Psychiatrist.

CHAPTER 6

___

FAITH

December 21, 2014, was a typical Saturday morning in Libertyville, Illinois. After enjoying a cup of coffee, working out, and walking the dog, I headed out the door for my weekly visit to my local barber—and everything typical came to a screeching halt.

As I jumped into my Infiniti QX4 SUV, I reflexively grabbed my seatbelt, just like I do every other day without thinking about it. On this day, however, I heard a soft voice in my head: *Don't buckle your seatbelt.* Even now, all these years later, I still can't believe I simply dropped the seatbelt and started the car, since that is something I would never ordinarily do. But at the time, I didn't question it and just backed out of the driveway, heading down MLK Drive toward the barbershop in North Chicago.

About two-and-a-half miles from home on a four-lane boulevard, as I was crossing through a green light at an intersection, a semi-truck pulling a trailer ran the red light heading straight at my side. The same soft voice I had heard in my driveway said, *Lay down across the passenger seat. You're going to be OK. Lay down.* So I immediately threw myself all the way down and blacked out.

When I came to, I was pinned down in my sideways position in the wreckage, my SUV sandwiched beneath the trailer part of the 18-wheeler. The roof of my car was crushed and nearly completely torn off. The headrest of the driver's seat had been completely sheared off. From what seemed like far away, I could hear sirens and people saying, *I think he's dead! He's decapitated!* Miraculously, I was in fact alive, and I was rescued from my vehicle.

Because of the severity of the crash, I was rushed into an ambulance and immediately transported to the nearest hospital, where they put me through numerous x-rays and CT scans. Incredibly, I had nothing broken, no cuts—not even a scratch!

A police officer who came to the hospital to discuss the crash told me, "An angel was with you today." She explained that if I had been buckled—like I am literally every time I get into my car—I would have died. The seatbelt would not have allowed for me to lay down across the passenger seat.

I believe it was Divine intervention that preserved me that day. I believe it was my faith and relationship with God that saved my life. On that particular day, it wasn't my time. There was more for me to do.

Only Faith

In this brief chapter, I'll be sharing a little about my faith and how it shaped my entire career experience. My faith played an integral part in the experience, but if you would rather not hear about it, you can move to the next chapter. I'm not trying to push my own faith on you, but I would be negligent if I failed to talk about it, because I believe there will come times in everyone's career and life when only faith will see you through.

Going back as far as I can remember, faith and church were important to my family. My grandparents were devout Christians. As I mentioned earlier, my dad even became a pastor. For us, church was not just on Sunday; it was several times during the week. We prayed at home often as a family. Julio and I went to Bible study, choir rehearsal, worship services—church life was just part of our daily life.

I gave my life to God at a very early age, so by the time I left home for college, and then later in the military, I was pretty well-rooted in my faith foundation. There were times in the Army when I started to feel challenged by some of the hardships and the obstacles I was encountering, to the point that I felt like I needed some help.

When I'd call home to my mom and dad to express my frustrations, they'd ask, "Where's your faith? Have you been to church?" I'll admit that when the going got tough, I had strayed away, but their nudging got me back on track. I started going to church again consistently. My faith really guided my walk of life. The challenges and obstacles became easier because I knew someone was with me; God was watching over me. I knew I was going to be safe and felt like my life was being used for a purpose.

In 1990, the first Gulf War was the largest deployment of soldiers since Vietnam. Even though I was prepared to potentially pay the ultimate sacrifice, my faith and connectivity with God never wavered. I knew without a doubt that I would see my family again because I prayed and asked God for His grace and mercy. I felt that my purpose in life was to be a blessing and inspiration to others whose faith may not have been as well-grounded as mine.

After my time in Desert Storm, things got shaky, and I fell off track again. Looking back, I now understand it was related to the PTSD symptoms I shared in the previous chapter. But back then, I didn't know what was going on. I would ask God to help me through it, but it didn't happen quickly. Yet even when I struggled in weakness, using alcohol to conceal and cope, I never doubted God's love for me.

Leaning into Faith

I believe God guided my corporate career path, too. By 1994, after leaving the Army and beginning employment with Kraft in Madison, Wisconsin, Bobbie and I were struggling to make ends meet. We were living paycheck to paycheck, primarily due to my poor career and job-change planning. As a result, my marriage was shaky. Frankly, it seemed the end of our marriage was near.

Finally, one day I got to the breaking point. I made up my mind to give things another few days, and then I would just have to quit my job and start a new career. Later that night,

I prayed and asked God to give me the strength to endure my challenges and give me the wisdom to make the right decision for my family. A week later, I was promoted from Operations Supervisor to Financial Analyst. I gave God all the glory and thanks.

In 1997, I was working in a Senior Financial Analyst position in South Carolina. My performance was outstanding, and I was considered to be a top talent in the company. However, because I wanted to inspire others and assist them in their professional development and career aspirations, Human Resources was the field that I really needed to be in.

I knew I couldn't reach my greatest potential and live my career journey to the fullest while in a Finance role. Even though I liked the prestige of being a Senior Financial Analyst, my heart and passion just weren't in that particular field. Even so, I wasn't seeking a career change. And at that time, it was unheard of to change your career path from Finance to Human Resources.

I prayed and asked God to work it out for me. Whatever direction and career He wanted me to pursue, that's what I would do. A few days later, Lyle, the Plant Manager, called me into his office, and, out of the blue, asked me to take on a special project for three months. He wanted me to lead an HR Recruiting Project focused on hiring Spanish-speaking Food Scientists and Engineers. I completed the project, and because of the great results, I was asked if I wanted to change my career from Finance to Human Resources. The rest of the story is the history of my career.

In 2012, Kraft split into two separate companies: Mondelez International and Kraft. All employees were assigned to one of the two companies. It was out of most employees' control; someone higher-up had already made the decision. However, I was one of the very few senior leaders who had the opportunity to select which company I wanted to join.

All of my long-time friends and colleagues were assigned to Kraft, which is where the old and dying products were assigned. Kraft was the only company that I had worked for, and it was all I knew. For those reasons, it was where I really wanted to go. On the other hand, Mondelez International, which was really Nabisco along with other international products, was a new company with vibrant brands.

One night, I prayed and asked God to give me the wisdom to make the right decision, "But better yet," I said, "God, let your will be done." A soft voice said *It is time to move on. Let the past go and embrace the future.*

My heart was heavy, and I didn't want to let go, but I had to. A few days later, I officially joined Mondelez International and eventually retired from the company. However, Kraft was soon acquired by Heinz and experienced a massive layoff. All of my long-time friends and colleagues lost their jobs; fortunately, most of them later landed jobs with other companies across the country.

This incident required me to step out on faith in a huge way, yet it persuaded me again that I could trust God to lead me.

Don't get me wrong, the biblical adage is true: Faith without works is dead. God is first in my life, and I didn't get to the top by myself, but I busted my rear to work hard. And my faith kept me grounded. Without it, my family and I would not have recognized that we have been so richly blessed over the years in every aspect of our lives.

My faith is still a top priority. I start every day reading from scripture or a daily devotion. I pray and self-reflect often during the day. I believe having deeply-rooted faith is key to success in life. In fact, I have anchored my life's work on the lesson found in Matthew 25:23 (ESV): "His master said to him, 'Well done, good and faithful servant. You have been faithful over a little; I will set you over much. Enter into the joy of your master.'"

Lean in to your faith for inspiration and encouragement on your own career journey, especially for those times when the going gets tough.

I pray you lean in to your faith for inspiration and encouragement on your own career journey, especially for those times when the going gets tough.

CHAPTER 7

FRICTION. DIVERSITY, EQUITY & INCLUSION

I returned to Madison, Wisconsin for the second time in July of 2003. I had been in charge for nearly a year when several positions became vacant in my department, one of which was an Associate Human Resources Manager that would report directly to me. I had an acute awareness of the lack of diversity in management positions across the company, and I recognized this was finally an opportunity to hire a person of color, but I refused to settle for anyone less than the best. One thing was non-negotiable: the candidate had to meet the job qualifications *and* be the right fit for the position.

I scheduled a meeting with the Plant Manager to provide my point of view and concerns regarding managerial diversity in the company. I told him it was important for me to lead by example, and it was my responsibility to find the best and brightest diverse talent to fill our vacant positions. It was another defining moment for me because I had to make a bold and courageous statement. By doing what was right, yet potentially unpopular, it meant that I was going to bust up the good-ole-boy club and raise the eyebrows of some of my colleagues.

The Plant Manager agreed with my decision and applauded my stand. He and I had worked together in California. Over the years, we developed a professional relationship that was built upon trust, respect, and accountability. Prior to accepting the promotion and moving back to Madison, we discussed why he had selected me for the position. He said that he knew I had high integrity, in-depth knowledge of the business, and could lead change in the workplace.

Several internal and external candidates applied for the position. During the interview process, members of the Leadership Team called and emailed me on different occasions. They strongly recommended—and sometimes demanded— who I needed to hire for the position. Of course, the people who they recommended were their close friends. Some didn't even have college degrees.

One candidate I encountered was a black woman who had over ten years in the company and an excellent performance record. April was a graduate of the University of Illinois and a prior resident of Madison. I met with her to discuss the position and to learn more about her experiences, successes, challenges, and career aspirations. It only took a few minutes for me to suspect April was the right person for the job. We then had an extensive conversation regarding expectations, leadership, agility, integrity, values, and accountability.

Before I offered her the position, she said, "Charlie, I understand that this is an important decision. I'm asking you for an opportunity to prove myself. I promise not to disappoint you, the Leadership Team, or the employees." I could sense her deepest sincerity. I clearly understood she was in the minority on two counts: black *and* a woman. Nevertheless, she was eminently qualified and needed someone to give her an opportunity and believe in her abilities.

That moment became an epiphany. I realized that at different stages in my career, someone believed in me, gave me a chance, placed a bet, and invested in my career. The time had come to seize the moment and pay it forward, level the playing field, and leave a legacy, not just for this person but for other people of color who would come after me. My decision made the company a better place.

I have friends from all races and orientations, so it's important for me to address diversity, inclusion, unconscious biases, micro-inequities, and microaggressions in today's workplace, not only through my personal lens as an African American man, but also through the lenses of others. Over the years, I've had many rich conversations with friends, both male and female, from a wide variety of ethnicities and other identifiers. What I share here are topics they would open up about to me to share how they felt. Sometimes it was my privilege to mentor them; sometimes they mentored me.

Overcoming Biases

Work ethic was important in my family. Most of my family members did not work in a corporate environment; they were what are commonly called blue-collar workers. My parents taught me to work twice as hard as the other guy and perform twice as well. Additionally, they taught me to get to work on time, look and dress the part, and let me know that hard work would get me promoted. These are values and beliefs that we also passed down and instilled in our kids.

While working in Corporate America, though, I learned that working hard didn't teach me how to advocate for myself nor promote my accomplishments. I learned early in my career not to take a passive approach. At times, I had to be my own advocate, but I never talked about what *I* did, just what *my team* did. I might talk about how developed they are, who's ready for promotion, what our results have been, and so on. Because I led them, they were a reflection of me (a concept I learned in the military). If a team is delivering, developing, and getting promoted, someone is behind that; it's not just happening by accident.

Yet the indisputable reality is that you can work hard and advocate for yourself all day long, but if you are a minority, you're often going to face additional barriers. Today's Diversity and Inclusion programs are working hard to eliminate those barriers, but there's still a long way to go.

I think race was a factor in my career when I started in 1993 with Kraft. However, I made up my mind not to let my ethnicity, color, or the company define me. I made it my mission to outwork and outshine everyone. In most cases, I was the first one in the office and the last one to leave.

During the mid-90s at Kraft, diversity hiring was a top priority. I believe Kraft was a trailblazer and leader in diversity, particularly in the Food/Consumer Packaged Goods Industry. Kraft had very few employees who were people of color when I was hired. Of the handful that were hired, most were African American; very few, if any, were Latino, Asian, or Indian. As a result, Kraft focused their hiring practices on bringing in a broader spectrum of qualified people of color.

We had a strong business case for diversity and did a great job supporting a diverse work environment. However, at this time, minorities could only go so far up the career ladder, and a chance at shattering the glass ceiling was nearly impossible. If you worked hard, performed at a high level, and consistently delivered great results, you were well on your way to make it to Mid-level Manager, but you would likely never reach the next level or positions of greater responsibility.

I felt that being the only minority on the team or in the room gave me the opportunity to show my skills and abilities. I saw it as a chance to show I could compete with the best, stand out, and shine in the spotlight. Most importantly, it gave me the opportunity to be a role model for others, even though it was a lot of pressure on me and a heavy burden to bear at that time.

There were undoubtedly some negative biases that I had to overcome:

1. **The Prove It Again Bias** – I did a great job and delivered results once, but could I do it consistently? I felt that because of the color of my skin, some people thought my success was a fluke that couldn't be repeated. So I had to constantly prove it over and over again.

2. **The Tightrope Bias** – I did not get the opportunities to fail or have a redo like other people, so I had a shorter rope. Other people had more freedom to try and fall short, but not me. Again, I felt this pressure due to the color of my skin. I couldn't afford to fail and get away with it because my rope was kept tighter.

3. **The All Eyes Are on Me Bias** – I felt like I was being watched all the time. As a result, I had to bring my *A-game* every day. I felt like if I didn't look busy, people would think I wasn't essential. So no one ever saw me just drinking my coffee and wandering down the hall. Even when I used the restroom, I tried to look like I was going somewhere important so no one would think I was slacking. I was being watched because of who I was, and I had to learn to live with that reality.

For the most part, people in my friend circle embraced diversity; we were raised in diverse communities and had a progressive mindset. For example, one of my close white male friends was the Plant Manager in California. We discovered we both came from humble beginnings: him from the projects in Brooklyn, New York, and me from rural Mississippi. We both worked hard to get our positions.

While he acknowledged that, as a white male, he likely had fewer obstacles to deal with, he did find himself feeling frustrated and overlooked when the company began to embrace diversity hiring as a *Focus on what you can control.* top priority. However, he shared with me that he learned to focus on what he could control and to give up worrying about things beyond his control. That was wisdom I took to heart and returned to again and again.

Even to this day, it's some of the best wisdom I can give people who think the deck is stacked against them—focus on what you can control.

Women in the Business World

Women in corporate America, no matter their race or ethnicity, undeniably face hurdles that their male counterparts generally do not. Yes, they are making progress; however, based upon the numbers in 2020, only 7.4% (37) women are CEOs of Fortune 500 ranked businesses, and only three of these women are women of color.[7] I was fortunate to work for a company where hiring women into the workplace, in general, was a priority. Still, the priority was not so much on hiring them to go directly into senior leadership roles.

One of my white colleagues shared that, in her experience, being a woman was often a negative, because in a historically male-dominated industry, senior managers and stakeholders were—you guessed it—white males. She even had one manager tell her she was hired because she looked good—something it's safe to say no male has ever heard from a manager.

Two other women colleagues, one Asian and one Latina, confided to me that they knew their race most likely gave them an edge in being hired, given the emphasis on bringing in a more diverse staff. One of the worst-kept secrets in corporate America HR is that hiring a woman of color lets you check off two items on the diversity and affirmative action checklist. However, both of these friends were very vocal, and when they asserted their opinions, they were called b-names (bossy, and the one that rhymes with rich).

Aside from the crass name-calling, they felt frustrated because their male colleagues, exhibiting the same behaviors, were often labeled as go-getters or deliverers. Men who are aggressive tend to be more tolerated in the workplace, and that behavior doesn't necessarily hinder their ability to move up the corporate ladder like it often does for women. I share these realities not to endorse them, but to prepare you for what you might encounter.

Kraft was better than many comparable businesses in its focus on promoting women into leadership positions. For over a decade, we had one of the most competent CEOs within the Fortune 500, the highly-talented Irene Rosenfeld. At that time, Kraft was a model organization for women. It appeared women were given opportunities within the organization based on their talent, and several held top positions in HR, Quality, and Supply Chain.

Even so, there were times when I had to speak up and get involved in situations where women didn't get opportunities for reasons completely unrelated to their skills and talents. Maybe they recently had a baby, or had a young family, and would have to travel significantly in a new position. Rather than having a conversation with the woman to find out where she actually stood prior to making a decision about her possible promotion, the manager would often make the hiring or promotion decision based on what he imagined she would want or be capable of. Thinking he was helping her out, he would award the position to someone else, ultimately derailing the woman's career trajectory. A little candid communication, not assumptions, can go a long way in these matters.

Prior to exiting the company, I recall speaking with a close friend who is a white male. He told me that women in general were treated differently and judged differently than men. Color didn't matter. In the mid-1990s to mid-2000s, he said they used the term TWM (Tall White Men) to describe individuals who were at the highest levels of the company. Sad, but true, all the senior leaders and top positions in Kraft at that time were TWM until the mid-2000s.

How Old Are You?

When it comes to diversity, inclusion, unconscious biases, micro-inequities, and microaggressions, one element that's often overlooked, yet an issue in most organizations, is ageism.

This is especially true if there's a reduction in force (RIF) or formal succession planning practice. When that happens, it's an unwritten core practice to identify, develop, and promote junior talent, usually someone forty and under. It's a method of getting rid of older, higher-paid employees and replacing them with much younger, cheaper talent.

In most companies, the magical age seems to be 55. If you're 55 and have 10 years of service, you may be one of the first to go. The company could potentially bring in two or three younger people for the equivalent of your salary. To be fair, they're running a business and have to consider if paying you next year will give them a Return on Investment (ROI).

Some companies tend not to hire employees over 50 because they are considering the future needs of the organization. They often want someone who will grow with the company, who they can develop, who has the greatest potential, and from whom they can receive the greatest ROI.

As the CEO of your own career, be intentional about making yourself so valuable that when cuts happen, your name isn't on the job elimination list.

However, in some industries, this practice is slowly changing since employees are staying in the workforce longer and often add value with their technical knowledge, professional maturity, and ability to mentor/bring along younger professionals. If you have a niche or hard-to-find skill set, sometimes larger companies will keep you on, or smaller companies will hire you. That being said, no matter the situation, it's of utmost importance that 50+ employees find ways to remain relevant in every way possible.

As the CEO of your own career, be intentional about making yourself so valuable that when cuts happen, your name isn't on the job elimination list.

Legal Action

Obviously, discrimination in the workplace for any of the above reasons is not legal. However, that doesn't mean it doesn't happen. If you feel discriminated against for any of these reasons, how can you actually be proactive when you're feeling like it could be a potential issue?

First, speak with your manager *if* that manager was not the offender, accuser, or enabler. If you don't see positive results, speak with a member of Human Resources or the Ombudsman whom you trust. I emphasize the trust part because, the reality is, they are people, too, with their own biases and existing relationships in the company. If that doesn't resolve the problem, you could always take your issue up with the EEOC (Equal Employment Opportunity Commission) or the Department of Human Rights in your state.

I would also advise doing what a colleague from many years ago taught me: if you seek promotional opportunities, spend your time and energy focusing on what you can control. There is discrimination in the workplace, some intentional and some not. Almost everyone has to deal with it to some extent.

You can choose to expend all your energy fighting the battle but losing the war, and sometimes it *is* the battle to fight, but other times, it may be best to change companies or careers and find an organization that will value what you bring to the table. You should research and understand your current or potential employer's Diversity and Inclusion goals, as well as how senior leaders are held accountable if the goals are not achieved.

> Discrimination is fought with facts and details, not emotion.

If you choose to fight the discrimination battle, be prepared with facts and data. You will get nowhere with phrases like, "They basically said..." or "I've been there longer." Discrimination is fought with facts and details, not emotion.

Understand that most career moves or promotions are not based on race/gender/age/sexuality, etc. Usually, it's because of who you know, the relationships you have, or the network you've developed. So, get to know some people who can help you get to where you want to go.

You cannot change or control what others do. You cannot change or control what others say. You cannot change or control how others treat you. However, you have complete control over how prepared you are for your work, how well you do your work, and for whom you work. If you are not appreciated for who you are where you work, take your talents elsewhere. Remember *you* are the CEO of *your* career.

THE CAREER LIFE CYCLE

EXPLORATION

I n August of 1987, after graduating as the #1 Officer in the Air Defense Officers Basic Course, I reported for duty as a Platoon Leader in the 1st Cavalry Division at Ft. Hood, Texas. In many ways, it was the beginning of my career. I wasn't wearing a corporate suit, but a different kind of uniform. My first day on the job, I walked into the Unit Headquarters wearing a freshly-starched battle dress uniform and brand-new spit-shined boots. I was a hotshot, the expert at everything, ready to give orders and command respect from my soldiers. CPT Jennings, my Company Commander, greeted me and requested that I meet with my soldiers.

Following several hours of getting to know my soldiers, I noticed very few of them were actually speaking to me. Later in the day, SSG Oatis, my Platoon Sergeant who had over ten years of military service, called me over to his work station.

"Can I talk to you in private?" He then said something profound that altered the course of my career. "Sir, you are our Lieutenant, our platoon leader. You make the decisions. But…you still have to earn our respect."

As his words sunk in, I realized that if I was going to succeed as a leader, I couldn't do it alone. I didn't have to be good at everything, but I had to empower others while holding them accountable. In that initial role, I needed this Platoon Sergeant's full support and trust. He had the knowledge, experience, and respect of every soldier in the platoon. Even though I earned a leadership position and title, I still had a lot of work to do—and a lot to learn.

Leadership requires intentional effort over time.

In that defining moment, I learned the meaning of leadership in the workplace. It is truly the art of influencing and bringing out the best in others to achieve a common goal, treating everyone with dignity and respect, regardless of their position.

And it doesn't just happen during your first day, week, month, or even your first year on the job. This level of leadership requires intentional effort over time. And that's why so few people at this stage take advantage of the opportunities to grow. They want to move up the ladder quickly, but, in their haste, actually slow their own growth.

Figuring It Out

The Exploration Stage is the time of early employment when an individual in their early to mid-twenties graduates from college and enters the workforce. The typical person in this stage usually has several fantasies and unrealistic expectations. I was the same way.

Like many college graduates just getting started, I believed that earning a Bachelor's Degree meant I was guaranteed a respectable salary and an executive position in Corporate America. Little did I know that my degree was only the price of admission. It got me a foot in the door, but that was it.

The lightbulb came on after Bobbie and I got married and I graduated from my ADA Officer Basic Course. When I got my first real paycheck with taxes taken out, I discovered there wasn't much money left. Not only that, but…surprise! I also didn't get to start at the top.

Nevertheless, as a 21-year-old, newly-commissioned 2nd Lieutenant in the US Army 1st Cavalry Division, I had a huge ego. I felt invincible, and acted like it, too. I had more than a slight chip on my shoulder, and I wore it proudly every day. After all, I had graduated in the top five of my ROTC graduating class at Jackson State University. I had been named top graduate of my officer basic course class. I believed that cliche: winning isn't everything; it's the *only* thing. I suppose I wasn't much different than most young, ambitious officers in the military, or the countless new hires I've seen in the corporate world over the decades.

To say I was impatient would be an understatement. I became a victim of the "I Want It Now" syndrome. It wasn't an easy pill to swallow that I wasn't appointed to every leadership position I wanted. When I didn't get picked, it really bothered me for quite a while. I felt that by graduating from college and my officer branch course with high marks, I was somehow entitled to be at the top or in key leadership roles.

However, after a seven-year career in the military, I ultimately learned that the necessary skills for being successful were persistence and patience. I came to understand that I wasn't ready and didn't have the experience others had who came before me, which was why I wasn't immediately put into advanced leadership positions.

It took a while because I had to battle negative thoughts. *Was I being held back because of the color of my skin? Did my commander just not like me?* Unfortunately, I entertained all kinds of negative thinking. The bottom line was, I needed to mature during that time but struggled to see it.

One thing I often failed to understand is that the Exploration Stage is the most forgiving stage of your career. My parents taught me to work twice as hard as everybody else, but I came to understand that it's okay to try hard and fail. It is *not trying* that is unacceptable. In fact, this stage of your career is an opportunity to fail early and often.

Everyone expects you to fall short when you are just starting, not so much once you reach the more advanced stages. As I came to understand this more, I consistently put in the hard work to be the best that I could be, utilize my God-given talent, and reach my full potential. Most importantly, I felt my time would come; it was only a matter of *when* it would happen.

A Straight Line Isn't Always Best

I worked my way through the Exploration Stage while I was in the military, but how would this stage look for a young person just getting started in a corporate environment or for an entrepreneur starting up a business? As a new entrant in the workforce, it's very important to understand career progression. How can you advance within your department? What is the company's organizational structure? What opportunities could there be outside of your department? Conversely, what do you need to learn as you grow this business? What mistakes can you afford to make? And are you preparing for the growth that will come as you succeed?

Once you understand the answers to these questions, you should be able to develop an idea of where you want to go and how to get there.

For example, when you're coming out of college and new to the Human Resources field, generally the first position you'll get is HR Assistant, then HR Associate, then HR Manager, then HR Associate Director, then HR Director, then HR Vice-President. So you have to understand the organizational structure and the developmental requirements at each stage in order to get promoted. With most companies, unless they are a small organization, the career path is fairly well structured.

However, the path you take to get there is not necessarily linear. The shortest distance between two points is a straight line, but in the business world, you may have to move laterally to expand your experience and build a solid career foundation.

Often, when college graduates enter the workforce, the primary focus is on the job position or title, rather than focusing on opportunities for cross-training, in-depth learning, and development.

In the Exploration Stage, I eventually learned that what's most important is where you end up, not where you start. You have to be a lifelong learner. Absorb everything you can learn from the position you are in. Become an expert on

> As long as you learn from mistakes, you'll grow from them.

as many positions as you can. This stage is your opportunity to soak up knowledge and experience, to try new things even if you fail occasionally. As long as you learn from mistakes, you'll grow from them.

One word of caution: New entrants into the workforce can be somewhat naive in thinking that all their colleagues or coworkers want to see them succeed. They may think, *Everyone is in my corner. Everyone wants to help me.* However, that's not how it works in corporate America, because in many cases you are competing with the people around you for positions. You have to learn who you can trust, who can give good advice, and who is a trusted team member.

That fact is part of what makes it so important to secure a mentor during this stage of your career. A mentor is someone to guide you and give you advice. A mentor is different from a sponsor, who is someone from within your company who chooses to help you advance. A mentor need not be in your company. In fact, at this stage, it's often more helpful to have someone who can offer you an outside perspective.

If you're new to the workforce, there are several methods you can use to find an appropriate mentor:

1. Join professional organizations. When I join organizations locally and nationally, I seek out those who can give me good advice about the industry, my profession, my job function, and leadership in general.

2. Connect with professionals on LinkedIn or other social media platforms.

3. Ask a co-worker or colleague in the workplace whom you trust (this is key!) and has several years of service or experience ahead of you.

4. Attend college or high school alumni events.

5. Contact a prior college professor or high school teacher.

6. Develop relationships in religious and community groups.

Wherever you find them, don't be afraid to ask for advice. The idea of grabbing coffee to gain professional advice is now the norm. The worst that someone can do is ignore your request or say no, but you'll never know if you don't reach out. Once the connection is made, you should set expectations upfront with your mentor on your goals for the relationship.

As I mentioned, you do need to keep a lookout when seeking a mentor from within your own company at this stage. The mentor/mentee relationship should not be forced. It should happen organically. It can't be based on the expectation of getting promoted or the appearance of favoritism. You also have to be careful not to be labeled as incompetent, incapable, or someone who merely wants something handed to them. Always be prepared to put in long-term effort to get the job done. Getting a mentor to help advise you may accelerate your growth, but it is not a shortcut to get out of hard work.

Unfortunately, in most companies, newly hired college graduates are expected to know how to navigate the corporate landscape. This expectation usually leads to anxiety and stress because you're left to figure it out on your own. There are a lot of unspoken rules you have to learn through trial and error, and failing to navigate them can derail you early in your career. That's why you can't be afraid to ask for help.

It's understandable that you might be nervous to ask for advice when entering a new role. You want to be perceived as knowing it all, but in reality, everyone knows you don't. You can easily become afraid to ask for help or admit you don't know something. But it's healthy to accept the reality that you don't know everything and are still learning.

You can't remain ignorant though. That's why you need to ask, quickly grasp the answers, learn the culture, and grow. But first, you have to ask.

Master's or Mastery?

Should I get my Master's degree before entering the workforce?
That's a question I get a lot from aspiring college grads.

Earning a Master's Degree is an awesome accomplishment. An advanced degree is usually required for upper management positions. However, without relevant experience to accompany the advanced degree, it doesn't necessarily equate to a higher salary or greater position of influence. The exception would be if you did an internship or had some sort of history with the company.

In general, I have found there's nothing more valuable than having a Bachelor's Degree and some experience *before* you earn your Master's, but it can also depend on the profession. If it's just a typical industry or company, I recommend getting your Bachelor's, getting some experience, then going for a Master's when you have the equivalent experience to go with it.

Your company may even be willing to pay for all or some of the tuition in that case. I recommend any person in Stage 1 of the Career Life Cycle look at the different companies' benefits for those who would pay for your Master's or your Doctorate down the road. For example, Kraft paid for my MBA about ten years into my career. I could have gotten it earlier, but because I was moving through the organization so fast, I didn't have time.

You choose which path is right for you, but more education without real-world experience may not produce the greatest growth when you're in the Exploration Stage of the Career Life Cycle.

Leadership Competencies

At each stage of the Career Life Cycle, individuals should have developed certain Leadership Competencies, which are skills and behaviors that contribute to superior performance. Your competency in—or ability to show—these skills will increase the trust that your team and your superiors have in you.

Though there are wide-ranging examples of Leadership Competencies, the five we will focus on for each stage of the Career Life Cycle are Personal / Interpersonal Skills, Drive, Strategic Skills, Operating Skills, and Professionalism.

LEADERSHIP COMPETENCIES IN STAGE 1—EXPLORATION:

Personal / Interpersonal Skills: Demonstrating self-awareness; self-development

☑ You are aware of your impact on others, as well as knowing yourself well and acknowledging that you have some blind spots.

☑ You reflect on what you have done, seek feedback, and are open to ways to improve.

> **Drive:** Action-oriented; drives results

☑ You have a strong sense of immediacy, focusing on the task at hand and seeing it through to completion.

☑ You consistently achieve results, even under tough circumstances.

> **Strategic Skills:** Business insight; mental agility

☑ You combine data and analysis to find meaning in and increase understanding of a situation, resulting in some competitive advantage for your business. This provides more than just a low-level understanding of an issue.

☑ You are able to think on your feet, solve problems, and are creative at work.

> **Operating Skills:** Plans and aligns; organizational savvy

☑ You are skilled at planning and prioritizing work to meet commitments aligned with organizational goals.

☑ You have become aware of and familiar with the often unspoken areas of organizational life, such as power dynamics, competing agendas, perceptions, turf issues, self-promotion, trust, and relationships.

> **Professionalism:** Situational adaptability

☑ You are aware of the complexities in a given situation and can be flexible and act differently when required because no two situations are exactly alike.

THE LIFE FULFILLMENT FRAMEWORK: STAGE 1—EXPLORATION

Family

When I started my military career, I was single with no kids. A few months later, I was married, and a few years after that we had our first child. In Stage 1, we should have discussed marriage and having kids in greater detail. Instead, things just happened!

Know that in Stage 1, you're sometimes required to relocate, which can cause unwanted anxiety and marital problems. It helps to have a conversation prior to marriage because having a spouse and family who are open to mobility is important.

> ☀ **Tip 1:** *If you're married, be intentional and discuss your family growth plans so you can know you are on the same page.*

> ☀ **Tip 2**: *Before marriage, discuss relocation. If already married, have that conversation now before you get asked to make a move.*

If both spouses have jobs and are career-oriented, someone will have to take time off work to care for a child or take care of important family situations. It's not that both of you won't care for the family, but it will require clarity on who takes the lead. And you don't want either of you to feel like you're alone during this hectic season of life.

Remember, the company doesn't love you, but your family does.

> ☀ **Tip 3**: *Find a family support group like daycare, church, or other social outlets.*
>
> ☀ **Tip 4**: *Discuss who will be the primary child and family care person.*

Trust is critical to build at this time, especially if one of the spouses is away from home on business or travels a lot. If one spouse becomes the primary breadwinner, his or her career priority can easily push aside important family relationships, creating stress and anxiety for both spouses.

> ☀ **Tip 5**: *Keep your family relationships front and center, even in the midst of important career challenges and demands. Remember, the company doesn't love you, but your family does.*

Financial

In Stage 1, I had to get over the unrealistic expectation that I could get rich while serving as an officer in the military. The reality became clearer when I exited the military and accepted my first corporate position with Kraft in Madison, Wisconsin. As a couple, we were living in the moment for several years, enjoying life, living from paycheck to paycheck. Saving money was not a priority. But Stage 1 is the perfect time to lay a strong financial foundation.

> ☀ **Tip 1**: *Develop a financial plan. Start small so you won't become overwhelmed.*
>
> ☀ **Tip 2**: *Start saving for retirement, even if it's a small amount. Get in the habit now and leverage any matching benefits your company offers.*
>
> ☀ **Tip 3**: *Learn how to budget your spending and savings. Take a course, seek a financial counselor, or study for yourself how to make and keep a financial plan.*

Fears & Challenges

At this stage of your career, your fears will likely be about failure or what people think about you. I struggled with fears of providing for my new family and how we would work it out in a way that would benefit our marriage.

You may wrestle with other issues depending on your physical makeup and emotional background. You might begin to see evidence of deeper issues that won't entirely surface until later, such as what happened in my own journey with PTSD. So be ready to seek help from advisors or professionals who can guide you through these challenges. As a general rule, the earlier you address them, the better.

> ☀ **Tip 1**: *Know that it is normal to have fears, so don't suppress or ignore them. Face them and discuss them with your spouse, trusted advisors, and mentors.*
>
> ☀ **Tip 2**: *Seek the help of a trained professional if you see signs of deeper emotional, relational, or mental issues. They will only increase if left unaddressed, causing more harm down the road for you and those you love.*
>
> ☀ **Tip 3**: *When you're embarking on any new career direction, expect to encounter a learning curve. That is normal. But if you don't expect it, the resistance you encounter may surprise and discourage you.*

Faith

When I was new to the workforce in the military, my faith remained the cornerstone of my existence. When I first relocated from Mississippi to Texas, I felt it was important to find a place to worship. However, finding the right place to worship and the right church family was a difficult decision because of the different denominations. We weren't looking for a perfect church, but we sought and found a church that met all our essential criteria.

I had a daily routine where I read a devotional that helped keep me in a great place mentally and spiritually. I was on top of the world at this point. I had my faith in action and my life on what I thought to be the right path.

> ☀ **Tip 1**: *Connect with a community of like-minded people who share your faith. For me, that was a local church where we not only got support for our faith, but also developed relationships that made us stronger.*
>
> ☀ **Tip 2**: *Have a daily routine designed to keep your faith focused and strong. Develop habits of prayer, meditation, or renewal that will keep you strong when the going gets tough in your career.*

Friction

In Stage 1, it's important to understand and embrace diversity. It should be a way of life. Additionally, you must learn to adapt to difficult workplace cultures, especially when you factor in mobility or relocation requirements. As you enter the workforce, you really need to have a clear mind and be able to deal with a wide range of diversity. If you don't embrace diversity, it may be difficult for you to advance and grow. At some point, your resistant attitude is going to be hard to cover up.

My time in the military was probably the most diverse experience I have ever had because it included working with people of all colors and languages. That diversity prepared me for similar diversity in my career.

As you advance in a company you might have to relocate. Cultural differences can come into play within different companies, departments, and even geographical regions. You have to adapt to those differences and thrive in them. You have to be willing to embrace differences and learn from them. If you can't operate and thrive in a diverse environment, it will derail your career.

You have to be willing to embrace differences and learn from them. If you can't operate and thrive in a diverse environment, it will derail your career.

When it comes to how others embrace you and your differences, you have to be confident in your own skills and abilities, even in the face of negativity. You have to accept that you can control only what you can control. You're not in it alone. If you run into challenges due to diversity issues, find someone you can talk to and have an open conversation about it.

☀ **Tip 1**: *Accept the fact that you can only control what you can control.*

☀ **Tip 2**: *Don't be quick to assume you didn't get promoted because of a diversity issue. After decades in the corporate world, I know most people don't think that way. Do a thorough self-assessment first to see what areas you have to learn and grow before assuming the worst of others.*

☀ **Tip 3**: *If you do conclude you are facing real diversity issues from others, find a mentor to talk to about your concerns, preferably someone outside of the workplace.*

☀ **Tip 4**: *The people in your own peer group may not be the best people to talk to about this because they can simply become an echo chamber.*

ESTABLISHMENT

In August 1993, I joined Kraft, Oscar Mayer Division, in Madison, Wisconsin as an Operations Supervisor. I was also selected to participate in their Pre-Management Trainee Program, a fast-track rotational program that prepared participants for future mid-level leadership positions in the company. The facility was a union manufacturing plant with nearly 2,500 employees, less than 1% being people of color.

In fact, there were only two black people in management: Shelia, a female Assistant Human Resources Manager, and me. She soon became my trusted ally. I was amazed at how she could work a room and was well-liked by everyone. She would often covertly contact me to ensure I was informed on key information. Eventually, our families became very close and lifelong friends. As the only black person in Production Management, I quickly learned the importance of building and maintaining strong relationships with my co-workers. Most of them were hard-working people who accepted me for who I was. They judged me based on my character, efforts, and results, not the color of my skin.

As any group does with a newcomer, though, they tested me to determine if they could trust me enough to be a member of their inner circle. My supervisor asked if I wanted to go deer hunting with him, the general manager, and a few other co-workers. I had hesitations about hanging out with a large group of men all armed with guns; however, I reluctantly said yes.

Before leaving the plant at the end of the day, my supervisor provided additional details, but he failed to disclose that we were going deer hunting in remote Northern Wisconsin. We headed for a small, secluded town to stay with an Amish family who had never seen a black person… in 18 inches of snow… in frigid weather, 2 degrees below zero. I began to ask myself, *What was I thinking?!*

Even though I was initially reluctant to say yes, the hunting trip was one of the best decisions I ever made. Thanks to years of military training and experiences, I proved my mental toughness, ability to work in teams, and willingness to adapt to different cultures on that trip. Most importantly, I earned the trust, confidence, and respect of my colleagues. The lifelong relationships I established with my co-workers placed my career on a thirty-year trajectory with the company that eventually led to a rewarding and comfortable retirement.

Opportunity Time

Stage 2 of the Career Life Cycle is the Establishment phase. At this critical stage, an individual is given opportunities to demonstrate agility, make mistakes, deliver results, lead at different levels, and receive promotions in positions of greater responsibility.

This stage usually starts around twenty-five years of age, and, in most cases, covers about ten years of an individual's Career Life Cycle. In some cases, the individual may be assigned a mentor or coach to assist in career development and advancement. In other cases, the individual may have to seek out such support.

My Establishment Stage occurred from 1991-1999, a time which included my last two years in the military, two years in Madison, and five years in South Carolina. I was always learning, test driving things, and volunteering.

After passing several tests (like the hunting expedition) and gaining my coworkers' trust, doors of opportunity started to open. After one year of service, the General Manager in Madison called me to his office and asked if he could be my mentor. That was a pivotal moment.

As I mentioned earlier, when we moved to Madison, there were less than 3% people of color living in the capital city. Hal was an older white male, former student-athlete, and UW-Madison alumni. It seemed obvious to me that he had been exposed to diverse cultures and different ethnicities. Most importantly, he seemed authentic and genuine.

He connected and scheduled a meet-and-greet between me and one of his close colleagues, who was a black male and the Human Resources Vice-President in the Oscar Mayer

Division. He asked him to teach me the ropes and ensure that I had the right contacts in Madison.

As my mentor, the General Manager required that he and I have a face-to-face meeting each month. He gave me monthly assignments to complete and required that I give him an update on what I had learned and accomplished.

Oftentimes, he asked how things were going with my wife and daughter. He would also ask how Bobbie was adjusting to the new environment and advised us not to hesitate to ask for help if we needed any support or assistance. He was instrumental in Bobbie finding employment at American Family Insurance Company.

I cannot express how grateful Bobbie and I were to have had someone who was at the highest level in the plant treating us like family. Because of the trusting, professional relationship we built and maintained, it allowed me to be totally engaged, bring my whole self to work, and perform to my full potential.

Having a mentor doesn't mean that he or she owes you a promotion or that you will get more opportunities. It is a chance for you to come alongside someone who can offer objective insights into what steps you might take and habits you might adopt to help you on your career journey.

I was fortunate that soon after I started working with my mentor—just a few weeks—I was promoted to a Financial Analyst position. We continued our mentor/mentee relationship, and I embraced and applied the wisdom and advice he so generously shared. After two years at the company, I was promoted to a Senior Financial Analyst position, which required relocating to South Carolina. At that moment, I realized something magical was happening, and the hard work was paying off. I was climbing the corporate ladder, and life was great!

When my plane from Madison landed in Columbia, South Carolina, I walked off the plane at the small airport into a warm, wet blanket of humidity. The South Carolina heat and humidity were suffocating. I noticed something in common with my home state of Mississippi—their state flag also had the Confederate Stars and Bars. I immediately felt a jolt of negativity about the state, worrying that it would be an upward racial battle the entire time I was living there, just as it was for me in Mississippi. I began to think twice about accepting the new position.

I rented a car to drive to the plant in Newberry, South Carolina, located forty miles north of Columbia. This plant was the polar opposite of Madison. There were 1,500 employees working at the plant, and most were black (60%) and Hispanic (30%). Fewer than 10% were white, which made me wonder what sort of experience I could expect.

After arriving, I met Lyle and Keith, the Plant Manager and Operations Manager. At this point in my career, I was comfortable, confident, and the color of my skin wasn't anything new. I was dressed to impress in my dark blue suit, starched white shirt, power red tie, and wingtip shoes. I had done my homework on the plant the night before and was prepared for the interview.

Lyle asked me one question: "Are you the guy from Madison who was sent to us by the General Manager to fill the Senior Financial Analyst Position?" When I replied, "Yes," he responded, "Then why are we wasting time with an interview? He called us yesterday to give us the 411. You are our guy. We are going to take care of you."

After finishing what he had to say, Lyle shook my hand and said, "Welcome to the team." Keith immediately assigned the Quality Department Supervisor as my Peer Buddy. My new buddy was an African American male Food Scientist who was extremely knowledgeable in food processing and operations. He and I learned that we had a lot in common and soon became lifelong friends.

Making Mistakes

At the Establishment Stage of the Career Life Cycle, you're still learning, growing, and making mistakes. If I was feeling a little too big for my britches because of this promotion, I was very soon brought back to reality.

My degree is in finance, not accounting. Yes, I took accounting classes in college, but I was far better at analyzing financial results and understanding where the gains and losses were coming from than actually *doing* the accounting in journal ledgers. However, not wanting to appear ignorant or incapable on any level, when a situation occurred that required some ledger work, I went ahead and tried to do what I thought I was supposed to, rather than asking Jim, the Plant Controller, for help.

When the end of the month arrived, and it was time to close out the books, I found out just how bad a move that was. About 7:00 pm on what was already turning into a late night, Jim came out of his office and said, "I wish we could be finished, but someone did a bad entry and we're $50,000 short."

I made the connection right away. I had messed up. I started sweating bullets, thinking I was about to lose my job. This guy was rigid, as are most accountants. So I had to go in and own up to it. "Jim, I have some bad news. I'm the one who screwed up that entry. I must have put the numbers in the wrong columns."

He checked it, and after we spent a couple of hours looking for the entry and how it impacted the bottom line, it was clear how I had screwed up. I had a team of analysts who worked for me who were good at this sort of thing—and I should have recognized that fact and handed the task over.

I probably lost some credibility that day, but at least I didn't lose my job. There is still some room for error during the Establishment Stage, and I was certainly grateful for it.

Experiencing Success

On another late evening, after finally closing the books in the Accounting Department for another month, the

Administrative Assistant walked over to my cubicle and said the Plant Manager would like to speak with me. A meeting with him was not an unusual request, since he reviewed my financial report each month during the Monthly Leadership Team Meeting.

The Administrative Assistant and I had formed a strong professional relationship and agreed to watch each other's backs. Prior to walking into the Plant Manager's Office, she grabbed my shirt and said, "Come here! I need to talk to you before you go into the office." She revealed that the Plant Manager respected me a lot, and then she proceeded to drop two bombs on me: he was going to ask me to lead a project, and after the project was complete, he was going to ask me to be a Plant Associate Human Resources Manager.

"You had better say yes," she urged. "You are a top-ranked supervisor in the plant. You can do it!"

I was speechless. My head started to spin. I had no idea how to be a Human Resources Manager! The Controller and I met the Plant Manager in his office. He said that the Human Resources Department was having trouble recruiting the best and brightest talent. As a result, the Leadership Team needed me to lead a three-month project to recruit, hire, and retain bilingual talent, specifically in the areas of Food Science and Engineering.

My first thought was that they were using me for something I really wasn't qualified to do. I could not remain silent and asked, "Why me?" I also asked if I was failing to meet expectations as Sr. Financial Analyst, believing this to be the only reason I would be put into a whole new department.

The Plant Manager said, "You are actually exceeding expectations in your role. You're one of our top talents at this plant. We just need your leadership and creativity in this role, and you can go back to the Accounting Department in three months if you wish."

Suddenly, I remembered what the Administrative Assistant told me prior to walking into the Plant Manager's Office. I took a deep breath, remained calm, and accepted the temporary position.

Over the next few days, I selected three individuals as members of my project team. Of course, I selected the Administrative Assistant, because I needed someone on the team who I could trust and who had excellent administrative skills. In addition to her, I selected two experienced Operations Supervisors: a woman from South Carolina and a bilingual man who earned a degree in Food Science from the University of Puerto Rico.

With the team established, our strategy was to target the University of Puerto Rico. The university satisfied two key recruiting requirements: the prospective students had US citizenship, and many students were bilingual. Little did we know the company had never considered any universities in Puerto Rico as a key recruiting pipeline. We were the first in the company to dream of this crazy idea.

As a result of our hard work and out-of-the-box thinking, the completed three-month project left us with eight new hires. All were bilingual supervisors from the University of Puerto Rico, and were made up of five Food Scientists and three Mechanical Engineers. The program we developed became a huge success and caused a lot of buzz across the organization. Ultimately, the company adopted our project as the first National Key School Program in Puerto Rico.

The success of this project resulted in a telephone call from Terry Faulk, the CHRO of Kraft Foods. He requested an in-person meeting with me at the Headquarters Office to discuss the National Key School Program and most importantly, he wanted to discuss my career aspirations. My meeting with Terry was pivotal and the ultimate game changer, which led to a career move from Finance to Human Resources.

Learning Agility

With my success and failures, I was learning—and learning agility is a key component of the Establishment Stage. You must be willing to take risks, be vulnerable, and be prepared to fail early and often. Additionally, you have to aggressively seek out development opportunities and assignments. You have to be strategic in seeking "key" growth opportunities that will enhance your skills and abilities.

That's basically what I did. I felt empowered to try things, to take risks. At one point, Joe, my manager, sat down with me and asked where I wanted to be in twenty years. He said,

"I want to help you get there, wherever it is you want to be." I put two things on that list: VP of Finance or VP of Human Resources. I believed I could do it. I had a vision. Joe told me he would do all he could to help me achieve it. I was eager to learn, so I was given opportunities. At this stage, it's critical to get your manager's and leadership team's support.

I consider myself to be a lifelong learner. I was always inquisitive, adventurous, creative, and never hesitant in providing my perspective. Additionally, I felt that my life purpose was to actively seek opportunities to be a trailblazer—I wanted to be first! I really never thought that I had reached my full potential. As a result, I did not accept complacency. And, yes, I was somewhat impatient.

When experiencing new or unfamiliar situations, I would always ask *Why* questions to gain a better understanding of situations, problems, or opportunities. Then, I would follow up with *Who, What, When, Where,* and *How* questions.

Learning was a skill I picked up in the military, probably due to the training I went through as an officer. They put you through scenarios where you have to think and plan for the future. When you're in a war, you're planning a battle, and each battle takes you closer to the end of the war. They build upon each other. When I was navigating through my career, I was looking at it as if I was on a mission, planning a battle to win a war. When you're planning for a battle, you're always thinking about how you can leverage Phase 1 to reach Phase 2.

Back then, I didn't know this type of thinking was called Learning Agility. In fact, I didn't know that specific term until a few years ago when I was a director at Kraft, but I've always loved the principle; I love what it does.

During my last two years in the military, I changed careers from Air Defense Corp to Quartermaster Corp. I was able to quickly adapt leadership skills learned in an all-male combat arms organization to lead in a diverse, mixed-gender Quartermaster organization. During the first seven years with Kraft, I was promoted four times, led several cross-functional projects, and relocated twice. Learning Agility is the ability and willingness to learn from experiences, and then apply the knowledge gained to perform successfully in new situations. It's all about adaptability, embracing change, and being able to see possibilities. Additionally, I earned my MBA while working full-time at Kraft, as well as certifications in Strategy, Diversity, and Personality Assessments.

I was already a director, so I really didn't *need* the MBA to get to a higher level. I did it for myself because I'm that guy. I'm always wanting to learn. Equally important, I wanted to stay relevant. I wanted to be able to compete. I did not want the organization to exclude me because I didn't have something.

What I've seen is that the higher up the corporate ladder you go (in most cases), at some point senior leaders will start to look at differentiators between you and your competition. What excludes you? Oftentimes, the lack of an MBA becomes an excluder. I owed it to myself to stay relevant, and I knew I could do it.

At this stage, you should be a lifelong learner, always wanting to stay fresh, stay competitive, and challenge yourself. So I'd recommend yes, go get that degree. If you think you don't have time, you have to make a commitment, exercising dedication and discipline. You must have a conversation with your manager—not to get his or her approval, because that's your business. But you want your manager's support. You want his or her blessing. There will be times when you have to take off work early or need some help with things, so you'll want that support. Get your manager's vote of confidence.

Ideally, you will work for a company that pays for that degree, as I did. But if getting an advanced degree is what you really want to do, with or without the company's support, do it. Do it for yourself. At some point, if you decide to leave the company and you have your Master's degree, it will help you at the next company. In fact, for some companies, it's the price of admission.

This Establishment Stage may not always feel like the right time to go after a Master's degree. In most cases, the next stage, the Elevation Stage, is the better stage to do it, because you've been around long enough that you have more practical experience to go along with the degree.

LEADERSHIP COMPETENCIES IN STAGE 2: ESTABLISHMENT

Leadership Competencies continue to build over the course of your career. The competencies of Stage 2 include continued development of the competencies introduced in Stage 1, as well as the addition of new skills and abilities.

> **Personal / Interpersonal Skills:** Self-awareness, interpersonal savvy, builds networks

☑ You build and maintain solid working relationships with colleagues, superiors, and direct reports.

☑ You continue to enhance skills such as good listening, empathy, honesty, sincerity, a strong orientation toward teamwork, trustworthiness, supportiveness, and a willingness to share responsibility.

☑ You develop formal and informal relationship networks inside and outside the organization.

> **Drive:** Drives results, resiliency

☑ You adjust to change, whatever the circumstances may be, and navigate all the ups and downs and twists and turns on your career path.

☑ You persist in the face of challenges and setbacks.

☑ You always keep the end in sight; put in extra effort to meet deadlines.

Strategic Skills: Business insights, mental agility

☑ You consistently apply a business driver and marketplace focus when prioritizing actions

☑ You are the first to spot possible future policies, practices, and trends in the organization, with the competition, and in the marketplace.

Operating Skills: Plans and aligns, decision quality, communicates effectively

---

☑ You actively seek input from pertinent sources to make timely and well-informed decisions.

☑ You think critically and make high-quality decisions, even when based on incomplete information or in the face of uncertainty.

☑ You develop and deliver multi-mode communications that convey a clear understanding of the unique needs of different audiences.

> **Professionalism:** Situational adaptability, courage

- ☑ You pick up on the need to change personal, interpersonal, and leadership behaviors quickly.
- ☑ You address difficult issues, saying what needs to be said.

THE LIFE FULFILLMENT FRAMEWORK: STAGE 2—ESTABLISHMENT

Family

When we moved to Madison in 1993, we had to depend on each other. There were no pre-established family, friends, or support groups in the area. We quickly learned that no matter where we lived, we had to support each other, enjoy family time, and never take our family for granted.

Additionally, I was extremely ambitious, and career advancement was a top priority. Often, I was away from my family due to long workdays, which included being the first one in the office, the last one to leave the office, and weekend work in the office. This stage will test the strength of your marriage and family unit.

> ☀ **Tip 1:** *Support and understanding from your spouse is critical. This means clear, two-way communication about expectations. Show that you're listening to their needs, too.*
>
> ☀ **Tip 2:** *This can be a chaotic time. Plan for how you're going to navigate the chaos. Build a support group and some type of outlet to just be a family.*

Financial

In this stage, *financial* is about more than just saving money or budgeting. We had to get more intentional in the planning process, particularly in how to navigate through purchasing a home and participating in the company's 401k.

The first substantial financial plan we discussed was buying our first home and how to come up with the down payment. We asked our parents to assist with a down payment, but they said no. Their advice was for us to figure out how to get the money.

We sharpened our pencils by eliminating unnecessary spending and paying off credit cards, all while allocating a percentage to our 401k.

> ☀ **Tip 1:** *Monitor spending in this stage by identifying Needs versus Wants. This is a time for short-term Wants to take a back seat to those longer-term financial goals, like homeownership.*

With every home that we bought, the company provided our mortgage loan at a very low-interest rate. Later, when the company came to us to relocate, they'd buy the home if it didn't sell within a certain time frame, so it could be a lucrative situation once you got into the groove. They provided a stipend, and if you were frugal, you could save some of that money.

> ☀ **Tip 2**: *Understand the company's policy around relocation and maximize it to your benefit.*

I was told when I moved from South Carolina to California that I would be in that role for about two years. Because of the timeframe, Bobbie and I needed to do our research and buy a home in a great location that could resell quickly. So we found a home in a progressive, hot-selling development that we knew could sell fast and make a profit.

> ☀ **Tip 3:** *Pay attention to resale factors (location, school district, etc.) when purchasing a home if you know you likely won't be living there long-term.*

Fears & Challenges

In this stage, personal challenges, adversity, and fears exist but are often ignored or subdued. I was overly career ambitious and refused to accept or deal with the problem at hand. At the time, I really did not know or understand my medical condition with PTSD. I would intentionally overlook symptoms to remain focused on driving results, meeting company goals/objectives, and climbing the corporate ladder.

I was afraid if I focused on my problem, stopping to deal with it, I would be distracted from my main goal. I was afraid someone would get ahead of me on the career track.

⚜ **Tip 1:** *Don't ignore your fears or challenges; confront them. See a therapist, doctor, or another expert who can help guide you through.*

⚜ **Tip 2:** *Share your thoughts and feelings with your spouse or family support system so they are aware of your situation and can walk through it with you.*

Faith

Faith continued to be important during the Establishment Stage of my Career Life Cycle. At this stage, my strong Christian wife was invaluable.

Due to my focus on career and delivering company results, much of the time I was just plain tired and fatigued. As a result, it was difficult for me to build up enough energy to go to church. Nevertheless, my wife was my inspiration.

She kept me focused and always reminded me that we were blessed and should always be grateful for our countless blessings. Most importantly, we should never lose our faith and remember that God is always in control. She coached me to remember that although I may feel like the best-of-the-best at work, I should always keep in mind Who got me there.

> 🔆 **Tip 1**: *You may be tempted to disengage from your faith, but if you do, it's going to expose you to more fears, lead you to fall into bad habits, get more out of tune with your family, and live in a state of overwhelm.*

Friction

It's very important to understand how to leverage the *Power of Differences*. At this stage, you're in the first level of managing or supervising. We are all different, so the key is to have an open mind, finding similarities between yourself and others, and to focus on positive intent.

> 🔆 **Tip 1:** *Seek experiences that require you to step outside of your comfort zone, including relocating to a different city/state or seeking an assignment that requires you to work with different ethnic/multi-cultural groups.*

Equally important in this stage of your career is to realize that everyone who looks like you is not always your friend, and those who don't look like you are not always your enemy.

When I was in South Carolina, the majority of the employees were like me, African American. After being with the company for five years, this was the first time I had Black co-workers.

Initially, I was extremely excited about the idea of finally joining an all-black team, being role models for minority employees, and having a positive impact not only at the plant, but also in the local community. For me, this was a dream come true.

After several months in the Human Resources Department, I soon realized that some of my co-workers perceived me as a threat and as someone who they had to compete with for promotional opportunities. Even though I was able to excel in the role, I found the experience to be comparable to a bunch of crabs fighting each other in a bucket. Rather than being a cohesive unit, supporting each other, the engagement and interaction within the department became unbearable. This experience in the workplace can occur within any homogenous group, regardless of your race or nationality.

> *We are all different, so the key is to have an open mind, finding similarities between yourself and others, and to focus on positive intent.*

> ☀ **Tip 2:** *Cultivate friendships and relationships—in and out of work—to include people who don't look like you, think like you, speak like you, vote like you, etc. Keep an open mind.*

———

ELEVATION

After relocating to California and living there for several years, my family had gotten comfortable with being on the West Coast. The girls were happy and enjoying the beautiful home with a gorgeous swimming pool in the backyard surrounded by palm trees. I thought life could not get any better.

Then, Barry, the Plant Manager called me to his office to inform me of some unexpected news. He had been promoted to General Manager and was relocating to Madison, Wisconsin, the place where my career had started in the company. I was happy for him, even though I was a little sad that my friend was leaving.

Prior to his departure, he and I had lunch together one afternoon and he said, "Charlie, you're like a little brother to me. Even though I am relocating to Madison, my goal is to ensure your next role is an executive position that comes with a larger salary, bonus, and company stock. That's the level where the real money is made. Your body of work already speaks for you. You've earned a seat at the table. After I get settled in, I'm going to bring you back to Madison. You know the terrain, the union, and the people. I need you as my business partner." I agreed that it sounded good, but didn't think anything else of the conversation.

Three months later, I received a call from Ty, the Vice President of Human Resources (VPHR). He said, "Charlie, you are being promoted to an executive-level position. We need you to relocate from sunny California back to the frozen tundra of Madison, Wisconsin." (Yes, he actually said that.)

I took a deep breath, connected with my inner self, and remained quiet for a moment. For the first time in my career, I felt conflicted about a potential move. I felt compelled to consult with my family and ask for their support rather than making a one-sided decision. I wasn't sure if I was ready to uproot my family again and seriously disrupt their lives. After ten years in the company, I finally realized my career choices impacted my family. They deserved to be included in making the decision about whether to stay or go.

As it turned out, the VPHR was the previous Human Resources Manager at the Newberry, South Carolina plant several years prior to my tenure at that location—and he was black. Eventually, he became my mentor, sponsor, and lifelong friend.

After we finished talking, I received a call from the Plant Manager who had been promoted to General Manager: "Welcome to the team! I told you I was going to bring you back to Madison to be my business partner. Oh, by the way, you are a legend in Madison. Everyone knows Charlie Jones!"

And with that, the Enrichment Stage of my career had begun.

A Critical Time to Grow!

At this third stage of the Career Life Cycle, you'll have been in the game long enough to understand how it's played and to have earned a seat at the table. In most cases at this stage, it's simply unacceptable to fail to deliver results or to add value to the company on a daily basis.

You have proven in the previous Establishment Stage that you're learning agile, ambitious, and can deliver results. Stage 3 is the time to challenge your confidence and put your knowledge to the test. At this stage, you must have confidence in your own skills/abilities, be able to deliver top-tier business results, be comfortable competing with the best-of-the-best, and thrive on being in charge and leading people.

That said, it is also critically important to understand the business, have functional expertise, understand technical processes, embrace diversity, and get things accomplished by delegating to other people and teams. In order to be successful in the Elevation Stage of your career, you must have a strong foundation and meaningful experiences in the Establishment Stage.

The bottom line is this: if you don't handle this stage well, there won't be a Stage 4. I'm not trying to be an alarmist, but Stage 3 is the most critical stage; if you don't make it here, you're done. You've had the opportunity to fail in earlier stages, but doing so in the Elevation Stage could derail your career.

By this point, you must have embraced the reality that you are the CEO of your own career. You more than likely have an assigned sponsor and should be on track for promotion at least two levels above your current salary. If you've put in the time, worked hard, made connections, and delivered consistent results, you're probably considered to be a top talent at the company.

If you are an entrepreneur, your business has likely grown to a level of stability, and you'll need to make decisions as to how far you want it to grow and in which direction. You'll likely need to make trade-offs and choose key people to help lead the company for years ahead as it outgrows your ability to manage it all yourself.

At this stage, it's essential to balance career and personal life, because a lot will likely be asked of you in both directions. Plus, you should be well on your way with retirement savings, wealth building through 401k or other retirement vehicles, stocks, and personal savings.

Nothing Comes Easy

Some people have the misconception that the higher you climb on the business success ladder, the easier it gets. You imagine you'll just sit back and let those lower than you on the ladder do all the heavy lifting. The reality is just the opposite. The higher your position, the more responsibility you have, so by the Elevation Stage, you can expect to face challenging situations regularly.

As the first black person appointed as a Department Head, returning to Madison seemed surreal. I had a huge office on the third floor and a staff of twenty-five employees.

On day one of the job, several peers and co-workers stopped by to congratulate me, including the two Operations Supervisors who taught me everything I knew about the meat production industry. I also received a call from Joe, a man who used to be one of my mechanics when I was an Operations Supervisor.

Later that day, he walked into my office: "Charlie Jones, it's great seeing you! We've finally got someone on this leadership team who the people can trust, who knows this plant, and someone who I can work with. I am so glad management got rid of that last HR guy. He was a piece of work."

Uncertain where this conversation was headed, I asked Joe what was going on. "Charlie didn't they tell you?" he replied. "I'm the Union President." Historically, there had been tension between union leadership and company management. I was caught off guard because I never imagined my old mechanic would be the Union President.

As we discussed issues and concerns between the union and the company, Joe began to get out of control, and the conversation got heated. He got excited, slammed his fist on my desk, and yelled at the top of his lungs. Even though I asked him several times in a calm yet direct manner to please lower his voice, he continued his tirade.

At that moment, I reverted back to Captain Charles L. Jones, the military leader who had been dormant for nearly ten years. I ordered Joe to get out of my office immediately, or I would throw him out. I told him I wanted to work collaboratively with him, but I refused to allow him to act like that and talk to me in an unprofessional and condescending manner. I also told him that he was not allowed back in the plant until further notice. He and I both stood there staring at each other until the Security Officers escorted him out of the Plant.

A few days later, I received a call from Joe. He asked me if I could come to his office at Union Headquarters to talk. Prior to meeting with him, I thought it would be prudent to call a previous Human Resources Department Head to get some historical perspective and insight on the relationship between management and the union. Unfortunately, I got no help at all. In a demeaning tone he said, "Charlie, if you think that I am going to bail you out and do your job for you, you're wrong. You're supposed to be the hotshot. I think the job is too big for you. Figure it out yourself."

I wasn't expecting his tone nor his reaction. I kindly told him I was not looking for a handout, but I was expecting a helping hand. "I called you to gain a better understanding of the HR issues and concerns in Madison." I may have been a little too direct in my sarcastic good-bye: "Thanks for nothing, and have a great day."

When I walked into the Union President's Office, it seemed as though I had stepped back in time as a character in the *Godfather* movie. The President and the Union Steward were sitting behind the desk with their feet propped up and smoking cigarettes.

"Have a seat. Charlie, I apologize for my outburst the other day," he said. "There are some good people in management, and there are some good people in the union. I really think you're the guy to make this work, and you're the *only* guy I'm willing to work with." Then he added a cryptic warning, "Oh, by the way, watch your back; some people in management don't want you in your role, they wanted their buddy there instead."

I had already figured this out based on my interaction with the previous HR head earlier. I told Joe I accepted his apology and was willing to work with him, but we weren't going to always agree. It's all about respect and credibility.

Three years later, after restructuring the workforce into a more diverse and inclusive culture, and negotiating the most lucrative bargaining agreement in the company's history between the management and the union that saved the company millions of dollars, I received a call from the VPHR. He told me I was being promoted to Associate Director, Global Supply Chain. I would need to relocate to the Company Headquarters, located in the northern suburbs of Chicago, Illinois.

On my last day in the office, I received a call from the Security Office. The VPHR and his entourage made an unexpected visit to my office. We discussed my accomplishments and career goals. Afterward, he presented me with the Human Resources Organization Excellence Award, the highest honor that a Human Resources Professional can receive in the company.

While the visitors were still in my office, Joe, the Union President, also made an unannounced visit. He looked at the VPHR and said, "I was told that you are in charge of Human Resources in Headquarters." The VPHR replied, "Yes, I am."

"I have something to tell you about Charlie Jones," the Union President said. "He is the best HR professional that I have ever worked with in my forty years at this plant. He cares about people and is a man of integrity." Then, he looked at me and said, "Charlie Jones, on behalf of the Local Union, we want to give you this plaque to show you how much we appreciated your leadership and partnership with the union over the last three years."

I was both speechless and humbled. As I reflected upon all the hard work, long hours, and countless sacrifices made to get to this stage of my journey, it became quite an emotional moment for me.

Never Close the Windows

Do you recall the story I shared in Chapter 5 about the PTSD-triggered anxiety attack I experienced during my first presentation? Well, that event happened during this Elevation Stage shortly after I got started in my new role in Headquarters. And there's more to the story. After the PTSD episode, I lost my confidence. I slipped into a depressive state because I had never failed while giving presentations before. I wasn't eating or sleeping right, and just felt very down on myself.

One of my mentors, Diane, a senior VPHR two levels above me at the time, saw me in the company cafeteria about six months after the incident. She asked me to come to her office after lunch. When I arrived, she asked if I'd ever put my resume out in the marketplace. I said no, but wondered why she was asking. Was she telling me I needed to start looking for another job?

"You probably should put it out there," she said.

"Excuse me?"

"You should put your resume out into the marketplace."

"Ok...well, thank you." I was worried. I went to my office, got my bags, and went home. I told my wife, Bobbie, I had been told to put my resume out on the market. Her response was not surprising: "*What?!* Are you going to lose your job?"

"Apparently so!"

So, I did as Diane suggested. I put my resume out. I got some bites, and eventually—after about three months— received a fantastic job offer to work for a well-known company back in California. When I told Bobbie about the offer, she said she didn't want to move again. So, I kept looking.

That day when I went to work, Diane saw me and called me back to her office. "Did you do what I asked you to do?"

"Yeah..." I waited for the other shoe to drop.

"What happened?"

"I got a job offer."

"What?!" she exclaimed. "I didn't want you to accept another job!"

"Well, you told me to put my resume out!" I'll admit, I was totally confused.

"No, Charlie, you misunderstood. I wanted you to get an understanding of your value and your worth. I saw your head hanging down. This was my way to get you to understand your own value, to be confident in yourself and pick yourself up. Give me a hug! I don't want you to leave."

Well, I don't mind telling you that my confidence level went from below 0 to 100! I got my swagger back. I may disagree with the way she taught me the lesson, given all the unnecessary anxiety it provoked in myself and my family, but it worked.

The takeaway is, even in the Elevation Stage of the Career Life Cycle, it's a good idea to keep your options open. Keep a finger on the pulse of the marketplace, talk to headhunters, and do interviews so you always know your worth. Keep your name out there, because you never know what tomorrow will bring. Never close the windows of opportunity.

Never close the windows of opportunity.

The same is true for entrepreneurs. Always be open to new opportunities as you grow your business. You just never know what opportunities may develop when you have the mindset to look out for them.

The Succession Plan

If you are in the corporate world, most companies have a Succession Plan that is reviewed and discussed by senior leaders in the organization on an annual basis, usually late in the 3rd Quarter or early in the 4th Quarter. Individuals are not placed on the Succession Plan until they've reached a certain job title or pay scale level. Your manager and/or Human Resources should inform you of the process and let you know where you are on the Succession Plan. Your manager should have a career or talent planning conversation with you annually or semi-annually.

At this point, having a sponsor is so valuable. A sponsor is different from a coach or mentor. Rather than guiding and directing you on a regular basis, your sponsor is usually assigned to you or volunteers to be your *corporate godfather*, sometimes even without your knowledge. This person has a seat in the room when senior leaders are discussing who gets promoted or assigned to key and critical positions within the company, and will advocate on your behalf. They function like an invisible hand guiding the process.

Being placed on the Succession Plan generally happens when you reach a certain level in management and is typically based on potential and performance. It may be that you're well-placed where you currently are, or you may be considered top talent, the best and the brightest, and will be slotted for upward mobility.

At the Elevation Stage, you should be on the Succession Plan to be promoted to at least two levels above your current salary grade. When you rise to senior manager level, if no one is telling you that your name is listed on the Succession Plan, or your manager is not discussing succession planning with you, my advice is to ask.

When you sit down with your manager for your annual evaluation, ask directly if you are on the Succession Plan. Ask if you are looked upon as top talent, someone who has legs or a skillset to go higher up in the organization.

In my experience, if you're really doing what you need to do and are considered among the best and brightest, you really don't have to ask; they'll seek you out. But there are some people who are on the bubble, right in the middle, and don't really know their future. If this is the case, you may not be on the Plan, but you can't be afraid to ask.

If you've made it to that senior level, you must be courageous and ask your manager the tough questions. If you're a senior leader who doesn't feel comfortable asking if you are on the Plan, then you probably aren't.

If you do ask and find you're not on the Plan, you'll have to have a difficult conversation with your manager. Ask what he or she sees as your next opportunity. Does he or she see you having different opportunities or greater responsibilities in the organization? You can still have a good career if you understand that the likelihood of your moving up is slim, but you can move around laterally. But at some point in your career, especially if you know you're not going anywhere, you might have to make the tough individual decision that it's time to move on.

LEARNING COMPETENCIES IN
STAGE 3—ELEVATION

> **Personal / Interpersonal Skills:** Collaborates, values differences

- ☑ You build partnerships and work collaboratively with others to meet shared objectives.
- ☑ You recognize the value that different perspectives and cultures bring to an organization.

> **Drive:** Optimizes work processes, nimble learning

- ☑ You know the most effective and efficient processes to get things done, with a focus on continuous improvement.
- ☑ You actively learn through experimentation when tackling new problems, using both successes and failures.

Strategic Skills: Mental agility, strategic mindset, cultivates innovation

- ☑ You see ahead to future possibilities and translate them into breakthrough strategies.

- ☑ You map out aggressive steps that will clearly accelerate the organization toward its strategic goals.

- ☑ You create new and better ways for the organization to be successful.

Operating Skills: Dealing with complexity, change agility, delegation

- ☑ You make sense of complex, high-quality, and sometimes contradictory information to effectively solve problems.

- ☑ You address new challenges as they present themselves, rapidly implement and integrate new learning or practices, and even change an entire direction resourcefully within a short space of time.

- ☑ You provide direction, delegate, and remove obstacles to get work done.

- ☑ You convey clear performance expectations and follow up consistently.

> **Professionalism:** Manages ambiguity

- ☑ You operate effectively, even when things are not certain or the way forward is not clear.
- ☑ You adapt quickly to changing conditions.

THE LIFE FULFILLMENT FRAMEWORK: STAGE 3—ELEVATION

Family

After moving back to Madison, Wisconsin from California in 1999, I thought this time things would be a lot easier. I was wrong. First, we had to deal with the fact that our daughter, Tiffany, was struggling with relocating again, leaving friends and a school she loved. It took her about six months to adjust. Our other daughter, Eryka, was just young enough to think of the move as another adventure.

Meanwhile, my wife, Bobbie, left a wonderful job in the banking industry and had to start over again. Every time we moved to another state, it became clear that Bobbie was having an increasingly hard time finding jobs that matched her experience and salary requirements.

Tip 1: *Before committing to a relocation, sit down with your family and lay out all the pros and cons of such a move. If the cons outweigh the pros, you may need to consider other options.*

In order to succeed in my new role, I had to put in long hours that were taking away from the time I could spend with my family. Bobbie and I discussed ways for me to be more involved, even though I was burning the candle at both ends. I would schedule my last meeting of the day earlier to make it home for the girls' sporting events or school plays. We got creative with alone time (scheduling date night on Fridays). No excuses!!

Tip 2: *Calendarize your family priorities. Treat those appointments just as seriously as you do business meetings and other appointments.*

The important key: We were considerate of each other and made the effort. And it worked. I know my family made sacrifices for me, and for that, I am extremely grateful. Overall, my family gave me the support I needed to make it to the next level. I made sure the office knew my priority was my family, and I would make every effort to be there for my kids.

Financial

This stage is the beginning of financial freedom if managed intentionally and strategically. You should be financially sound by now and well beyond investing more than the minimum to participate in the company's retirement plan due to increased salaries, bonuses, and company stock.

> ☀ **Tip 1:** *Audit your current investment in your company's retirement plan. Meet with a financial advisor to discuss how to maximize this investment.*

There are other creative ways to gain financially, too. For example, we relocated three times with the company. During each relocation, we purchased a home and learned how to maximize the company's relocation program. For example, when we purchased a home in California, we ended up selling it at the peak of the big housing market bubble. We used that equity money to invest with our Financial Advisor.

This Stage is the time to begin building wealth. Maybe with your increased income, you'll want to buy some toys, like a big boat or a fancy car. But remember, there's always a tradeoff. Our choice was to reduce our spending, become debt-free, and save as much as possible so we would be able to enjoy life later on. Yes, if you wait until later, you're taking a risk. But I had faith.

> ☀ **Tip 2:** *Financial splurges you make today might be better invested in your future financial freedom.*

Fears & Challenges

It was during this Elevation Stage that my health condition was magnified. If you've been ignoring physical or mental challenges, or pushing aside fears and concerns, this is where it will probably all come to a head as the pressure increases. And when mine did, I knew I needed help. Don't be afraid to reach out and ask for that help. I was forced to deal with my reality at this stage, but in hindsight, I wish I had acted much, much sooner. When it became real to me, I accepted it and was willing to seek help. This advice can apply to any type of friction or obstacle or fear. I got medical and therapeutic help, and it made all the difference.

> 💡 **Tip 1:** *No matter where you are in the Career Life Cycle, when you recognize you are struggling with a particular issue, seek help. There is absolutely no shame in speaking to a counselor, doctor, friend, or mentor.*

Faith

During this Elevation Stage, my faith got stronger. I looked back over my life and saw all the successes and accomplishments I had achieved, and for which I was so incredibly grateful. I could see God's hand leading me.

My faith got even stronger as I became more active in the church and in the community. I became more of a role model and began to use my life and my story to help others. Understand that life is not perfect for anyone, no matter how good it looks from the outside. You're either in a storm, just coming out of a storm, or going into a storm. All the pressures and life challenges of this stage can stretch your faith.

> *Your faith can stay strong through all of life's storms if you decide to trust in God's plan, and know that if He brings you to it, He'll see you through it.*

I'm here to tell you that your faith can stay strong through all of life's storms if you decide to trust in God's plan, and know that if He brings you to it, He'll see you through it.

☀ **Tip 1:** *Don't neglect your faith and spiritual matters during this hectic, high-pressure season. Instead, lean into it and let it grow.*

Friction

At this stage, diversity is critical because now the organization is looking to you to set an example and put processes in place to help others succeed. It's my belief that as a leader, my success is not just determined by me, but by the people that surround me.

At this point in your career, you are likely in a position where you are managing a department and leading people.

> As a leader, my success is not just determined by me, but by the people that surround me.

You're in charge. If you have an opening in your department, you're accountable for bringing in diverse, well-qualified talent. The expectation is, by ensuring your team is diverse, you are helping the entire company become diverse.

🔆 **Tip 1:** *Look to HR to make sure you have a diverse group of candidates to select from when you're making hiring decisions. Additionally, annual goals and objectives at this level often include hitting diversity and inclusion goals.*

🔆 **Tip 2:** *Inclusion doesn't have a color or gender; it's all about including everyone, bringing everyone along, which is equally as important as diversity. Look for opportunities to help each and every member of your team reach their full potential.*

ENRICHMENT

started to read the tea leaves at Kraft in 2013 when I saw what was happening across the company with people being let go. In addition, the company's long-standing pension program, of which I was a part, was coming to an end. I recalled the old Russian Fable about the scorpion and the frog:

> *A scorpion asks a frog to carry him over a river. The frog is afraid of being stung, but the scorpion argues that if it did so, both would sink and the scorpion would drown. The frog then agrees, but midway across the river the scorpion does indeed sting the frog, dooming them both. When asked why, the scorpion points out that this is its nature.*

I started feeling a bit like the amphibian carrying the scorpion while my company was developing a stinger.

With all the signs that things were changing, and not for the better, Bobbie and I started planning. We decided to start a business—a side-hustle doing HR consulting—which wasn't in competition in any way with my current employment. To begin, we worked pro-bono with non-profits to build credibility and a reputation for our own new company.

Because I knew the end was probably near with Kraft, I actually felt more fulfilled in my life purpose working on my own project, versus working for a company that I felt was devaluing me. This new passion became my driving force and purpose. I knew I could do it. I felt needed. I felt my expertise was desired and added more value to these non-profits than to the company paying me a lot of money.

I also started to volunteer to serve on boards. I was on two local non-profit boards before I left the company. This service gave me the assurance that I was still adding value and had a greater purpose in life beyond the company, as I began to see all too clearly that the company did not love me. I needed that encouragement and inspiration, and I wanted to feel like I had a purpose outside of the company.

The details of your journey may change, but you should always keep an eye on what's going on at the company, think ahead, be proactive in a methodical, intentional way because you are the CEO of your career. That's what good CEOs do.

Reaching Your Peak

During the Enrichment Stage, you'll reach the highest position possible based on your career trajectory and promotability within the company, whether it is the company you started or an international corporation. At this stage, you're still loyal and you still have that fire in your belly, but at some point, you'll begin to read the tea leaves as I did.

Unfortunately, in most cases, position and salary stagnation occur, as there simply are not many higher positions for advancement. The air starts to get pretty thin. When you realize you're not going to be promoted further, or you've grown as far as you can in that environment, you have two options: stay and make the best of it or take a job with a different company where you can advance further.

If you stay, seek ways to remain relevant and add value. Ask yourself what you have done for the company lately. Do your best to have a strong professional relationship with your manager. People tend to see the company through the lens of their bosses or managers, and they stay or go because of that relationship, more than for the company itself.

Let's face it—at this stage of your career, ageism can become a concern. Age 55 and 10 years of service are important numbers, particularly as it relates to a reduction in workforce, cost savings, and the company's bottom line. Therefore, you can't stick your head in the sand to try not to deal with the inevitable. At some point in life, you will begin to reach the sunset of your career. However, that doesn't prevent you from focusing your efforts and attention on remaining relevant, exceeding performance expectations, and being a subject-matter expert. Not only can doing this make your journey fulfilling, but in some industries, employees are also staying in the workforce longer and often adding value with their technical knowledge, professional maturity, and ability to mentor/bring along younger professionals.

If you decide to leave, you must have a plan for your next move immediately. At this stage, you should always have a transition plan and an exit strategy ready because you don't know when you may be invited to leave.

If you haven't yet met with a financial advisor, it's definitely time. By this point, you need to know your target for retirement savings, both the dollar amount and the year you want to retire. Your trusted and certified financial planner will help you make sure you're where you should be.

Also during this career peak, you should *become* a mentor to help guide others through their career experiences and challenges. Spend time developing others to get them ready for promotions. I was very intentional in leaving a legacy through others and ensuring the company was seeded with the best and brightest talent.

During and prior to this stage, I aggressively sought mentees who were eager to learn, willing to put in the work, and committed to reaching their full potential as human resources professionals. I felt responsible for the future of the company, as well as the viability of the Human Resources function. I mentored several successful HR Professionals, some of whom are still with the company, and others who left for external promotional opportunities.

You'll also begin to prepare for life after your corporate career, laying the foundation for the life you want to live when that day comes.

Learn to Read the Tea Leaves

In the Enrichment Stage, you are getting closer to meeting the retirement threshold. During this stage, it's critical that you pay attention to the signs that reveal themselves.

If you are in a corporate environment, understand how the company operates, both its written and unwritten rules. Be attentive—know what's going on in the business and in your industry. Understand and know the details regarding major company changes, such as mergers, acquisitions, divestitures, and workforce reductions. Participate in the quarterly or annual company earnings meeting to gain a better understanding of the state of the company. You will be surprised by what you learn and the bits of knowledge discussed.

At this point, you are expected to be a subject matter expert (SME) and the go-to person in the company, or for your brand if you are an entrepreneur. You have long-tenured experience and a broad professional network. The company is expecting a Return on Investment (ROI). You will have to show your value and worth.

Remember that you're nearing the twilight of your career; therefore, you have to remain relevant to the changes in your business or technical environment. It's more about continued professional development rather than functional expertise, which you should already have.

My focus at this stage turned to leaving a legacy with my direct reports, colleagues, and company. I became even more intentional about leaving behind a nurturing culture, a family atmosphere that's a great place to work. I would ask myself daily, "Who can I share with? Who can I help?"

This stage is also a time where you have the margin to truly make yourself a top priority. Take time to schedule meetings with your Financial Advisor. Take time off with your family. Maybe there are some places you've dreamed of taking them to. You may now have the financial ability and accrued vacation to do so. For our family, I sat down with my girls and said, "You know, I worked so hard and spent hours away from my family for so many years; now, I want to do something special."

From that point on, we did something every year. I took my family on a trip to Europe—France, Germany, Amsterdam, and the United Kingdom. We went to Cuba. The Dominican Republic. Mexico. Jamaica. We took a Disney Cruise. For seven straight years before I retired, we traveled. I spent the money, and I was happy doing it. I also spent time with old friends from the military and college. We scheduled boys trips and met up in Chicago, Dallas, and California.

In short, I enjoyed life. I treated myself and my family because, at this stage, we were financially sound. Tiffany had graduated from high school, and Eryka had passed the age of ten. We'd plan the trip a year in advance and really enjoyed looking forward to it.

All of this was possible because I had done what I needed to do earlier in my career.

Where to Next?

As you start thinking about life after your current company, whether moving on to another employer, starting your own business, or retiring, there are some resources you can and should use to help you get on the right track.

If you're looking for further employment, research a good resume writer to help you get your resume ready for distribution. Write your resume to keep the focus off your age, and highlight your outstanding qualifications and experience. Make sure your professional online profile (i.e. LinkedIn) is current and up-to-date. If you haven't created one yet, it may be a good idea to recruit someone to help you with that. (If you have young adult children, they're a great place to start!)

Maybe you've dreamed of starting your own business— exactly what I did! The Small Business Administration is a great resource for those just getting started.

If you know that retirement is your next step, then this stage is when it's important to start getting those ducks in a row. One of the first things to do is schedule a meeting with HR and the Benefits Provider to better understand pre-retirement topics, including the company's benefits package, pension, and 401k.

You'll also want to do your research, meet with experts, and ask questions about the following: financial planning, retirement planning, social security, tax laws, best places to live for retirees, and how to stay active physically and mentally.

Do not lock yourself inside a bubble. Connect with other people who are close to retirement, retired, or in a similar situation. Plan to spend some time together or establish a support group.

Whatever you do, don't get caught in a depressive state thinking about your career coming to an end. Get out of that space quickly—if you're intentional, the best is yet to come!

LEADERSHIP COMPETENCIES IN STAGE 4—ENRICHMENT

Personal / Interpersonal Skills: Communicates effectively

- ☑ You model and encourage the expression of diverse ideas and opinions.
- ☑ You adjust communication content and style to meet the needs of diverse stakeholders.

Drive: Resourcefulness

☑ You secure and deploy resources effectively and efficiently.

☑ You get the most out of available resources and locate rare resources others can't get.

☑ You adapt quickly to changing resource requirements.

Strategic Skills: Mental agility, strategic mindset, managing vision and purpose

☑ You paint a compelling picture of the vision and strategy that motivates others to action.

☑ You instill and sustain organization-wide energy for what is possible.

☑ You show personal commitment to the vision.

Operating Skills: Develops talent, ensures accountability

☑ You view talent development as an organizational imperative.

☑ You consistently use multiple methods to develop others.

☑ You promote a sense of urgency and establish and enforce individual accountability in the team.

☑ You work with people to establish explicit performance standards.

Professionalism: Approachability

☑ You keep your tone warm and friendly, maintain eye contact, and don't get distracted.

☑ You listen to what a person has to say without interrupting them.

☑ You pay attention to your body language.

THE LIFE FULFILLMENT FRAMEWORK: STAGE 4—ENRICHMENT

Family

Our family life had stabilized by this stage, and now it was time to do things that we had dreamed about during the career journey. We finally had the time and money. Now is when you really can spend quality *and* quantity time with your family and do things together, like taking a dream vacation and traveling the world.

Now is also the time to slow down and appreciate things that involved the family that you may have taken for granted. It's time to nurture and cultivate family relationships.

> ☀ **Tip 1:** *Make a family bucket list of things you all want to do or enjoy now that you have the means. Then choose one and put it on the calendar.*

Financial

Your financial portfolio should be enriched by now. It is time to develop your transition plan from Enrichment to Exit. This is also the time to consider the initial planning stage for retirement. You could start researching how to become an entrepreneur and start a small business if that interests you.

> ☀ **Tip 1:** *Schedule some time with your spouse or significant other to discuss your thoughts and plans around the next stage of your journey. Brainstorm together all the different options you could consider, then over a period of time, reflect on what resonates best with you as your next step.*

At this stage. people often begin to go into debt with a larger home or a more expensive car, overextending themselves, and forgetting to place a priority on a nest egg for the future.

> 🔆 **Tip 2:** *As financial guru Dave Ramsey says, "Debt is dumb. Cash is king." Sure, you are earning the most you've ever earned at this point in your career, but you are that much closer to the day when you'll need it for retirement. Be smart, and only spend discretionary funds that are available after all your savings are fully funded.*

Fears & Challenges

My medical condition was under control and was no longer my primary fear or challenge. At this stage, the fear of not having enough money to support us in retirement became the priority, and it quickly became a stress point. Working closely with my financial advisor and having plans for a small business of my own went a long way in easing my fears.

> 🔆 **Tip 1:** *Face your fears head-on, as opposed to ignoring them or pushing them to the back of your mind. Then, take whatever steps are necessary to fully address and manage your fears.*

Faith

I began to lean more heavily on faith at this stage in my career. My career was stable; I was a known commodity, and my stock in the company was high (literally and figuratively). I felt more blessed and highly-favored than ever before. Most importantly, I gave God all the honor and glory for allowing me to be a faithful steward of my finances and talents. I knew this was all possible because of His grace and mercy.

Everyone to whom much was given, of him much will be required (Luke 12:48 ESV). If you have heard that line of wisdom, you know it means we are held responsible for what we have. If we have been blessed with talents, wealth, knowledge, time, and the like, it is expected that we benefit others. As a result, I gave back to the community by supporting ministries at my church, establishing scholarships for underrepresented graduating high school teenagers, and volunteering with my local fraternal organizations which include Phi Beta Sigma Fraternity, Veterans of Foreign Wars (VFW), Masons, and Shriners.

> **Tip 1:** *Make a difference in the lives of others and for the business. I can honestly say I made a difference for direct reports, the team, and the company. I nurtured, developed, mentored, and sponsored some amazing talents, five of whom are currently in Vice President roles in different companies.*

Additionally, I was at a point where I needed spiritual guidance to figure out the next chapters in my career. I flew to Mississippi to spend time with my mom and dad. I knew they would understand and provide the appropriate counseling since that's what they do.

Friction

In this stage, ageism becomes the focus. In most cases, opportunities are limited, and you will be passed over for promotions. It's very important to remain relevant and figure out how to ensure your talent is in high demand but in limited supply. Now is the time to reinvent yourself!

> ☀️ **Tip 1:** *There is no age limit on learning, so continue to learn and stay on top of the trends in your industry.*
>
> ☀️ **Tip 2:** *If you believe your expertise would serve a niche in another company, don't be afraid to explore that option!*
>
> ☀️ **Tip 3:** *Become a subject matter expert.*

EXIT

In 2013, when I reached twenty years in the company and was still in the Enrichment Stage of my Career Life Cycle, I began to aggressively seek opportunities within the company to remain relevant and connected to the right circle of influence. But I began to feel as though I was being passed over for opportunities. It wasn't until late 2016 to 2018, a three-year period, when I began to feel that I was being treated differently. As a result, I started to lose my passion and love for the company and began to second guess whether or not I had reached my peak.

From 2016 to 2018, I was a Human Resources Business Lead in the North America Sales Organization. But I began to realize it was a one-way love affair. So, more and more every day, my love became my side hustle, and working at the company was just my day job.

One October day in 2018, as I was working virtually from my home office, I received a call from my manager who I could immediately tell was crying.

"What's going on?" I asked.

She answered, "I have some bad news. I am so sorry."

I had a feeling I knew what was coming. I was waiting for it. I had planned for it.

After trying to pull herself together for a few minutes, she finally said, "We are going to have to sever you. I don't want to, Charlie, and I even raised my hand to volunteer to be let go instead, because I know how much you mean to this company."

I told her, "I'm going to be just fine. I have planned for this day, and it's going to be ok. But I'd like to know why. Why was the decision made to sever me now?"

She told me that she really didn't know. "What I was told was there was a huge restructuring, and several people have been impacted."

"Ok, no problem...so when is my last day?" When she said it hadn't been decided yet and that we could discuss it, I replied, "Look, let me help you out. Let's make the day January 1, 2019. Why don't you give me my exit paperwork on Dec. 31 or Jan 1, and give me a year of severance pay? Give me all the stock that I have coming. I'll be just fine."

It got quiet. I think she was expecting me to push back or be upset or angry, but I had planned for that day (I didn't tell her that) and as a result, I made her job easy.

What I didn't know was that for the vast majority of people who are let go, it's not that easy. They're not prepared. They don't know what's coming. I knew what was coming because I was reading the tea leaves. I knew the restructuring was coming and people were going to be let go. If I'm honest,

I have to admit I was hoping my name would be on the list. It was time for me to move on.

So, I told her to send me the paperwork, and I'd read through it and get back to her the next day. She emailed me all the documents.

When I opened the email, looked at the bottom line, and saw all the zeros before the decimal point, a slow smile spread across my face.

I immediately ran upstairs and shouted, "Bobbie, we got it!" I knew what the dollar amount was likely to be, and I knew the stipulations. Financially, I walked away smiling from ear to ear.

Pushing Past the Discomfort

I'm not going to lie, though, the emotional piece hurt, and in some ways still does. It's hard to swallow that I was let go with no real explanation. When I eventually got the paperwork and looked at a document called *Exhibit A*, my heart dropped. While my manager had been told that the restructuring had affected a lot of people, in reality, there were just two people on the severance list: a 63-year-old administrative assistant and me.

At that time we had 90,000 employees, and I was the highest-ranking African American in human resources. It really crushed me. I was extremely resentful that a person at my level in the company had been lied to. Even to this day, no one ever really told me the real truth about why.

I suspect I know what happened. We had changes in the Human Resources executive leadership team. A survey was sent asking if we felt the company was a good place to work. I wasn't a yes man. I was the guy that if you asked me a question, I'm going to tell you the truth. I knew that if I told the truth in this case, they may not want to hear it, but I went ahead. I also knew it could be the end of my career.

In my survey, I expressed my feeling that the current organization wasn't a good fit for me. I wasn't necessarily saying the company was bad, but that it was just different. I felt like to a certain degree, I was no longer adding value. It wasn't that I wasn't doing my job; I was just no longer having fun or enjoying my work. It wasn't the same family-oriented company as when I came on board twenty-seven years ago. Things had changed. We lacked the feeling that we're a team where people cared about one another. So no, in my opinion, it wasn't really a good company to work for.

I know that sounds foolhardy, responding to a non-anonymous survey like that, but in my position, I believed I was untouchable. I thought I had a bulletproof vest on. The truth is, I didn't really care all that much. My love and passion weren't with the company anymore; they were with my side hustle. I knew I could grow it.

A mentor once told me that if you can sleep well at night after a day of letting people go, then it's time to move on. And I had reached that point. In the last couple of years with the company, I didn't lose sleep. I got to the point where I wasn't caring as much about the people; it became more about the numbers in the company. I changed from a caring person to strictly business. It wasn't fun anymore. I knew it was time to move on.

So, no, I did not voluntarily exit the company. I was forced out, even though I never received a negative performance evaluation and always met—and usually exceeded— performance expectations. Over time, I learned not to take it personally.

It became another example of a truth I wish I had grasped earlier in my Career Life Cycle: *The company doesn't love you.*

You have a choice at the Exit Stage of the Career Life Cycle. You can either prepare to exit with dignity and on your own terms, or you can slip into decline. In the Exit Stage, the decision has been made, either by you or the company, that it's time to part ways, either voluntarily or involuntarily. If you're not prepared to step away from your corporate career and into what's next, this can be the most difficult stage. But it doesn't have to be. It certainly wasn't for me. You may choose to retire or reinvent yourself to remain viable in the workforce. Or both.

Here are some indicators that you've reached your peak in the company:

➤ Fewer opportunities are coming your way, and you sense a lack of promotability.

➤ You feel like you're not in the inner circle or circle of influence.

➤ You're not able to read the tea leaves because they're not giving you any tea leaves to read; you're out of the loop.

➤ You wake up in the morning, and you're not happy to go into the office or regret getting up to go to work.

➤ You really don't care about the company or your managers.

The Unplanned Exit

If the day comes when you are approached and informed that your job is being terminated, here are some things to keep in mind.

First, ask why the situation is happening. From a mental standpoint, it's important to understand so you can bring closure to your tenure with the company. Even though I suspect I know what prompted my severance, I lacked that official closure when I left Mondelez, and it made the transition more difficult than it needed to be.

Ask if the exit being presented to you is voluntary or involuntary. Do you have a choice in the matter? If it is voluntary, then you have to do some soul searching about whether or not you wish to stay with a company that may not keep you around much longer. At the very least, you will want to get your resume updated and put out some feelers if you choose to stay on.

When the exit is not voluntary, do your research and confirm if a severance package is being offered to exit the company. This package is not required, but it is a nice gesture by the company. With big companies, a severance package may consist of up to a year's pay, bonuses, stocks, cash-out of accrued PTO, professional transition services, and continued insurance for a period of time.

These days, as companies tighten their financial belts, a severance package is more likely to consist of two weeks of pay, whatever vacation you had coming, and COBRA healthcare coverage.

If some sort of severance compensation is offered, get a clear understanding of the total payout amount and benefits details, especially around healthcare insurance. Confirm the timing of the total payout amount due to tax implications. In other words, will the money be paid out in the current year or the following year, and will the payment be in a lump sum or dispersed during the regular payroll cycle? If it's paid during the regular payroll cycle, how many payments will be received? If a severance package is not offered, don't be afraid to ask for one. You have nothing to lose but everything to gain.

Find out if Professional Outplacement Services will be included in the severance package. This service will assist you and your spouse in transitioning and may include help with the job search, resume writing, and additional training.

Consult with an attorney and your financial advisor. When you get the severance package, there's often a severance and general release agreement that confirms the company is going to let you go, and, in return, is going to give you a certain amount of money or benefits. You'll be asked to sign this document saying you aren't going to sue them. If you don't sign the document, you don't get the package.

If you didn't read the tea leaves and you find yourself without a job late in your career, unprepared for the loss, there are some damage mitigation steps you can take. You may have to decide if you're going to officially retire and draw your pension, or if you're going to continue to work. It's important to discuss this with a financial advisor first to understand all the financial ramifications.

If you decide not to retire, then apply for unemployment benefits at your local unemployment office. Meanwhile, as you start a new job hunt…

➤ Update your resume.

➤ Seek assistance from an employment agency or recruiter.

➤ Leverage your professional network.

➤ Update your social media sites.

➤ Review and analyze your skills inventory.

Your unplanned exit is obviously going to impact your family, so I recommend scheduling family counseling to help you work through the transition, which can include a reduction in unnecessary spending and possibly downsizing, if necessary. It won't be an easy time for you or your family.

If the unplanned termination is thrust upon you, don't become the victim. Own it. Accept the exit. You'll be stronger by letting go and focusing on the future. Not letting go creates anxiety in several ways—mentally, emotionally, and financially—and it's just not worth it.

What's Next?

Many people have to work well into their 60s for their social security benefits and other financial reasons. This could put them in the Exit Stage for longer than ten years. Is it possible to have a meaningful work life when you're waiting longer to retire? Absolutely!

In that extended scenario, I would say you are extending the Enrichment Stage rather than moving to the Exit Stage and lingering there. You'll want to seize every opportunity to stay relevant by continuing to learn and grow in your role. Becoming a mentor is really a must-do in this scenario; you have much wisdom and experience to share, and the pleasure you'll gain by helping those behind you reach even greater heights is immeasurable.

However, you should definitely be using the extra time to ensure you are totally prepared to exit the company on your own when the time comes, following all the guidelines I shared in the previous chapter. And you have to stay prepared for the unexpected termination discussed above; remember, the company doesn't love you and is probably not concerned with whether or not you are financially ready to go. Your financial future is simply not a priority for the company. Be accountable for your own destiny.

Whether you retire, exit intentionally, or are simply let go without notice, the day will come when you wake up without your day job and think, *Now What?!*

First and foremost, it is a golden opportunity to spend some quality time with friends and family. If your financial situation is compromised, then don't worry about things like meeting up for lunch or playing an expensive round of golf; invite them over for a cup of coffee. Host a pot-luck dinner. You can have fun together and enjoy one another's company without breaking the bank.

Volunteer your time and services to organizations you care about, including nonprofits, churches, etc. I mentioned in the last chapter that I offered to serve on the boards of some organizations that are important to me. Your wisdom and expertise at this stage of your career may be exactly what a charity or other non-profit organization needs.

Connect with others in your age group or similar situations. In my case, when I exited the company, I really didn't know what to do. I was feeling a little lost. One day, I went to the golf course on a weekday and was a little surprised to find that there were actually many other people out there. I was by myself, and the only black person out there that time of day. A group of guys called out, "Hey— who are you? Are you golfing by yourself? Come on and golf with us!"

As we got to talking, I shared that I was recently retired. These guys, all older and also retired, started to tease me about being too young to be retired. They also discovered that my golf game wasn't exactly up to par.

That was many months ago. Now, every Monday and Thursday our group has a set tee-time. These guys have really taken me under their collective wing, and we have become friends. I'm learning things from them about golf and about retired life. They've become like friends.

LEADERSHIP COMPETENCIES IN STAGE 5—EXIT

Personal / Interpersonal Skills: Self-awareness, self-development

- ☑ You take consistent action to develop new skills that may serve beyond your current career.
- ☑ You are aware of the skills needed to be successful in different situations.

Drive: Ambition, nimble learning

- ☑ You enjoy the challenge of unfamiliar tasks.
- ☑ You seek new approaches to solve problems.
- ☑ You identify and seize new opportunities.

Strategic Skills: Mental agility, strategic mindset, business insight

☑ You have an in-depth understanding of how businesses work and make money.

☑ You formulate a clear strategy and map the steps that will clearly accelerate you toward your post-exit goals.

Operating Skills: Cultivates innovation

☑ You move beyond traditional ways of doing things and/or push past the status quo.

☑ You explore new, creative options for utilizing your skills.

Professionalism: Manages conflict

☑ You anticipate conflicts before they happen based on knowledge of interpersonal and group dynamics.

☑ You find common ground and drive to consensus, ensuring that all feel heard.

THE LIFE FULFILLMENT FRAMEWORK: STAGE 5—EXIT

Family

It is important to include the family in critical conversations because your exit affects not only you, but the entire family. Together, you should have a clear vision of what retirement looks like: whether you'll relocate, buy a retirement or vacation home, buy land, live close to children/grandchildren, etc.

> ☀ **Tip 1:** *Communicate with your spouse and/or family members constantly. Everyone should know the master plan. There should be no surprises at any point in this process.*

Financial

Consult with your financial advisor more often than in the past. Get a clear understanding of your total retirement savings and total expenses.

> ☀ **Tip 1:** *Know your number—the amount you need to be able to live comfortably for the rest of your life.*

> 🔆 **Tip 2:** *Focus on becoming debt-free if you're not already, and don't incur additional debt through unnecessary spending, like buying a new car or other high-ticket items.*

Fears & Challenges

The primary fear at this stage is the fear of the unknown or not knowing what's next. No matter how carefully and thoroughly you have planned for your Exit Stage, there is always some amount of discomfort when facing change and uncertainty.

> 🔆 **Tip 1:** *Embrace the fear or anxiety as normal. Everyone experiences it.*
>
> 🔆 **Tip 2:** *Lean in to friends or family members who've already walked this walk, and share your feelings and concerns with them. They may be able to offer their personal perspective on how they navigated this change of life.*
>
> 🔆 **Tip 3:** *Instead of viewing the Exit Stage as an end, view it as a new beginning, a chance for you to start all over with another version of the Career Life Cycle as you begin your next endeavor, whatever that may be.*

Faith

Faith and church were critical at this point. I would say this time of uncertainty was the biggest test of our faith as a family. We didn't know what was going to happen; we felt like we had enough money to do this, but we had never lived through it before. In fact, our parents had never lived this. Most of our family members were blue-collar people who didn't have the retirement options I had, so they had no experience we could draw from.

So, we really had to walk out on faith, and we tried to use our lives as proof to others that if we could do it, they could too. We wanted to inspire others to have more faith.

> ✺ **Tip 1:** *Trust God and His promises. Jeremiah 29:11(NIV) says: "For I know the plans I have for you," declares the LORD, "plans to prosper you and not to harm you, plans to give you hope and a future.*

Friction

The primary concern at this stage is accepting retirement. After getting up and going to work every day for 30-plus years, suddenly finding yourself without that daily obligation may cause some feelings of loss.

☀ **Tip 1:** *Look into activities geared towards retirees in your area. You'll be amazed at what goes on during the week that you never knew about when you were busy in the corporate world.*

☀ **Tip 2:** *Commit to a volunteer engagement that requires you to be in a certain place at a certain time each week. This will give similar predictability to your schedule as you are accustomed to from your 9 - 5 workdays.*

MOVING FORWARD

A s I write this conclusion, it's nearly the end of 2020, a year that I think we can all agree has been as unpredictable as any we've ever lived. And yet, despite the challenges, pivots, and uncertainties, thanks to my many years of dedication to the Career Life Cycle and my careful Stage 5 Exit plans, my new venture, C and B HR Consulting, is thriving.

After a career spent honing my expertise in Human Resources, I decided to partner with my brilliant and talented wife, Bobbie, to create an HR consulting firm that will help our business clients reach their full potential by building incredible, diverse teams and leaders. I consider it not just another job, but a calling, almost a ministry, to give back and inspire others.

There is something extra sweet about partnering with new businesses who are excited to learn about the solutions we can offer to help them grow their companies, but who also become our valued friends. That level of relationship and partnership is what I dreamed of when we started this firm as a side-hustle, and I'm looking forward to living that dream through the remainder of my working years.

My goal for this book is to be a beacon of hope for readers. If I could succeed in my career, even coming from my very humble beginnings, surely you can as well. The true test of a person's success is not just looking at where the journey started, but where it ends. With the right attitude, faith, and a lot of hard work, you can accomplish amazing things—things you may never have even dreamed were possible. Believe in yourself.

But you can't get there alone. In all my years interacting with people at the highest level of their career, not one has reached that point without plenty of help along the way, and my hope is that you will take the guidance offered in these pages to help you through the remaining stages of your Career Life Cycle, too.

If you're a leader in your organization and want your people to understand the Career Life Cycle and mindset, the Leadership Competencies, and the Life Fulfillment Framework, I would be honored to have a conversation with you about how you can leverage the concepts shared in this book to grow your team. Just visit CBHRconsulting.com and send me a note.

ABOUT THE AUTHOR

C harles Jones is the CEO and Co-Founder of C&B HR Consulting. The family-owned company was established in 2013 to provide human resources strategies and solutions to small businesses, nonprofits, and veteran-owned businesses. Some current clients include the Girls Inc. of Greater Houston TX, YWCA of Lake County IL, Pride & Hope Family Services in Varnado LA, and Millennium Corporation in Washington DC.

In 2017, he received the Lake County, IL Most Influential African American in Business Award. Prior to establishing his company, he served as a human resources executive with Mondelez International (formerly Kraft Foods), headquartered in Deerfield, IL. In this role, he was responsible for developing and leading the implementation of human resources strategies and activities in support of North America Sales with net revenues exceeding $6 Billion. Prior to his final year of service, he was the highest ranking African American in the Mondelez International human resources function.

He began his career with Mondelez as a Financial Analyst in Madison, WI. He transitioned into human resources in 1995 and has since held a variety of human resources assignments in Wisconsin, South Carolina, California, and Illinois. Several of his previous leadership roles include HR Director, Oscar Mayer Division, HR Director, Cheese Division, and Director Staffing & Diversity Global Supply Chain. Prior to joining Mondelez International, Mr. Jones served six years as a US Army Officer. He reached the rank of Captain and is a Iraq War Veteran.

Charles has served on several boards including the YWCA Lake County, University of Illinois – Lake County Extension, March of Dimes Lake County IL, Oak Grove School Education Foundation, INROADS of Chicago, 100 Black Men of Madison WI, and YMCA of Madison WI. He is also a Life Member of Phi Beta Sigma Fraternity Inc. Charles is a native of Mississippi. He earned a BS in Finance from Jackson State University and an MBA from Lake Forest Graduate School of Management. He is married and has two daughters.

Special Note about PTSD from Dr. Janet Taylor, Psychiatrist

Post-Traumatic Stress Disorder (PTSD) is a mental health condition that occurs in 7-10% of Americans but may often be misdiagnosed. PTSD can occur after an individual experiences trauma directly or witnesses a life-threatening traumatic event, like being in combat, living through a natural disaster, terrorist attack, car accident, sexual assault, serious medical illness, or severe emotional and physical abuse. PTSD is twice as common in women and can also be diagnosed in children and teenagers.

Symptoms of PTSD include re-experiencing symptoms of past trauma. Triggers can be sounds, thoughts, emotions, and even smells. Reminders of the trauma can lead to flashbacks, nightmares, and thoughts that cause fearful sensations. Another symptom is avoidance. People will stay away from people or situations that trigger memories of their trauma. Doing normal activities may be more difficult or left undone because of uncomfortable feelings that create a change in behavior. There may be patterns of distraction to avoid having thoughts and feelings that are unpleasant.

To avoid thinking or remembering, negative coping patterns like using substances to numb feelings can create more problems. Symptoms such as being easily startled, reactive, or constantly feeling on edge, unsafe, having difficulty sleeping, or irritability are common with PTSD. Changes in mood, concentration, feeling guilty, blaming others, and trouble remembering can also be frequent.

Everyone who is exposed to trauma does not develop PTSD. There are occupations that place people at a higher risk for developing PTSD because of exposure to high-trauma work conditions. It used to be thought that only veterans and military servicemen and servicewomen developed PTSD. Now we know that anyone can have a stress disorder after exposure to trauma, but if symptoms last longer than a month and result in social, work, educational, or daily living impairments, then the diagnosis is more likely PTSD. It can occur with other psychiatric diagnoses, and because of its impact on overall functioning, should be treated.

Treatment includes medication, talk therapy, or psychotherapy, as well as teaching families how to identify symptoms and be supportive of each other. If you have been exposed to trauma and have symptoms of extreme anxiety, flashbacks, re-experiencing, and reactivity to triggers, talk to a healthcare provider. SAMHSA, Substance Abuse and Mental Health Administration, has a National Hotline 1-800-662-HELP (4357) and provides a free, confidential 24/7, 365 day a year consultation in English and Spanish. Veterans with PTSD can call 1-800-273-8255.

ACKNOWLEDGMENTS

Anything of quality is usually the result of a team effort. Together with my loving family, mentors, trusted confidants, and lifelong friends, we have created something truly meaningful. I would like to acknowledge the following people who have been instrumental in my life, especially those who provided inspiration and encouragement, not only during the creation of this book, but throughout my career.

I want to thank my father and mother, Rev. Dr. Sidney Jones and Velma Jones, for your love and wisdom. You taught me how to dream big, put God first, and walk by faith. You have always been my beacon of hope, inspiration, and my example of the true meaning of love.

Thanks to my beautiful wife of thirty-three years, Bobbie, for showing me unconditional love and support. I cannot adequately express my sincere gratitude and appreciation. You make my life complete.

To Charlie's Angels, my wonderful daughters, Tiffany and Eryka, for helping me understand the importance of a father's love in ways I have never imagined. You're my joy.

And to my brother, nephew, and cousin, Julio Jones, Mario Jones, and Jimmy Joiner for your honesty and encouragement. You always keep it real.

I want to thank my mentors and sponsors Ty Bonds, Terry Faulk, Dorria Ball, James Atkinson, John Triplett, Stephanie Smith, Greg Buban, Kevin Jennings, Herman Jefferson, Hal Smith, Kwame Salter, and Diane Johnson-May. My success is a result of your guidance and inspirational leadership.

I want to thank the Talent and Organizational Development Professionals, Armin McCrea-Dastur Ph.D., Barbara Durant Ed.D., Colleen O'Toole, and Steve McIntosh. Your incredible knowledge truly brought my book to life.

I want to thank the Medical and Mental Health Professionals, Janet Taylor MD, Reginald Spears MD, and Tyree Brinson PsyD. Your expertise has been impactful in understanding and coping with personal fears and challenges.

I want to thank Barry Haberman, Deb Basler, Rick Harris, and Sheila Milton for your friendship, encouragement, and for being my sounding board. You challenged me to do my best work and provided diverse viewpoints.

I want to thank my personal confidant and advisor, Rev. Roy Peeples for being my friend, coach, and teacher. You have been my emotional safety net.

I want to thank Kevin Jennings, CEO of Millennium Corporation and Treopia Cannon, former CEO of YWCA Lake County for believing in us as new entrepreneurs and giving us our first HR consulting contracts.

ACKNOWLEDGMENTS

I want to thank the many trusted confidants and lifelong friends for providing wisdom, knowledge, and wonderful memories: Mike Page, Monique Page, Dietra Jennings, Jay Pope, Beth Pope, Joe Larson, Lyle Olson, John Munz, Kevin Jordan, John Milton, April Clincy, Quincy Woodard, Wallace Henley, Daniel Ferrere, Jim Dent, Rod Christmon, Demetris Crum, Dee Gibbs, Dex Mack, Corwin Harper, Dr. Carter Womack, Tom Abbott, Dr. Jose Restituyo, Kevin Chedda, Dr. Julius Dudley, Nailea Curiel, Andrew Lochner, Elaine Vong, Alexia Debrosse, Joe Wilson, Lisa Wilson, Karl Braun, Judy Braun, Keith Wolaridge, Kelvey Wolaridge, Stephan Marshall, Tom Celley, and John Marshall.

At StoryBuilders, I want to thank Bill Blankschaen, Jenifer Truitt, Akemi Cole, Kelly Sundstrom, and Stephanie Beaver for bringing my dream to life and to the global marketplace. Without your extraordinary expertise in coaching and editing, this book would not have come to be. You are committed to excellence.

Finally, and certainly most of all, I give all the glory, honor, and praise to my Lord and Saviour Jesus Christ for all that I am.

ENDNOTES

1. "Press Releases: The Conference Board." *Press Releases | The Conference Board*, www.conference-board.org/press/pressdetail.

2. Backman, Maurie. "Job Hopping: Why Millennials Resign Nearly Twice as Often as Older Workers." *USA Today*, Gannett Satellite Information Network, 11 June 2018, www.usatoday.com/story/money/careers/employment-trends/2018/06/11/why-millennials-resign-more-than-older-workers/35921637/.

3. https://www.shrm.org/resourcesandtools/tools-and-samples/toolkits/pages/developingemployeecareerpathsandladders.aspx

4. "Differences Between Employers and Workers Can Be Hurtful." *PLANSPONSOR*, www.plansponsor.com/differences-between-employers-and-workers-can-be-hurtful/.

5. Malik Lee, managing principal at Felton & Peel Wealth Management. "Black Households Try to Close Wealth Gap by Chasing Higher Returns." *CNBC*, CNBC, 20 May 2019, www.cnbc.com/2019/05/17/black-households-try-to-close-wealth-gap-by-chasing-higher-returns.html.

6.   Staff, DiversityInc. "Report: Black Americans Have
     High Financial Literacy In Some Areas, Scored
     Lower In Others." *DiversityInc*, 14 Jan. 2020, www.
     diversityinc.com/financial-literacy/.

7.   Ebrahimji, Alisha. "Female Fortune 500 CEOs Reach
     an All-Time High, but It's Still a Small Percentage."
     CNN, Cable News Network, 20 May 2020, www.cnn.
     com/2020/05/20/us/fortune-500-women-ceos-trnd/
     index.html.